SECURING TALENT

Securing Talent: Building and Retaining High-Performance Cybersecurity Teams by Dr. Kevin Lynn McLaughlin, offers a comprehensive and insightful exploration into the critical role culture plays in the cybersecurity field.

Dr. McLaughlin, drawing from his extensive experience in cybersecurity leadership and risk management, addresses the acute shortage of cybersecurity professionals and underscores the importance of a supportive work environment in attracting and retaining top talent. The book begins with a personal anecdote illustrating the significant impact of organizational culture on employee engagement and leadership development. It then delves into the global scarcity of cybersecurity professionals, intensified by the increasing complexity of cyber threats and rapid technological advancements. This shortage poses a considerable risk to organizations across industries, making them vulnerable to data breaches, reputational damage, and significant economic losses. Dr. McLaughlin emphasizes the necessity of creating a positive and rewarding workplace environment to not only attract but also retain skilled professionals.

The book discusses various factors contributing to the lack of qualified individuals in the field, such as inadequate investment in cybersecurity education and limited opportunities for skill development. Dr. McLaughlin argues that the high-stress nature of cybersecurity work, demanding long hours and intense focus, can deter potential talent. He advocates for investment in training programs, cultivation of the next generation of cybersecurity experts, and the creation of a workplace culture conducive to professional growth and satisfaction.

Kevin Lynn McLaughlin, PhD, is a renowned cybersecurity leader with over 30 years of experience in global security, risk management, and compliance. Throughout his career, he has led teams of more than 250 professionals, crafting and implementing world-class cybersecurity programs that protect critical assets, data, and reputations while driving business growth and resilience. Kevin's expertise lies in aligning cybersecurity initiatives with organizational objectives, delivering innovative and cost-effective solutions that meet the challenges of an evolving digital landscape. As an IEEE Senior Fellow, Kevin holds an impressive array of certifications, including CISSP, CISM, CRISC, CEH, GIAC-GSLC, and CCISO.

Security, Audit and Leadership Series
Series Editor: Dan Swanson, Dan Swanson and Associates, Ltd., Winnipeg, Manitoba, Canada.

The scope and mandate for internal audit continues to evolve each year, as does the complexity of the business environment and speed of the changing risk landscape in which it must operate. The fundamental goal of this exciting series is to produce leading-edge books on critical subjects facing security and audit executives and practitioners. Key topics addressed include Leadership, Cybersecurity, Security Leadership, Privacy, Strategic Risk Management, Auditing IT, Audit Management and Leadership, and Operational Auditing.

Agile Audit Transformation and Beyond
By Toby DeRoche

Information System Audit: How to Control the Digital Disruption
By Philippe Peret

Next-Generation Enterprise Security and Governance
Edited By Mohiuddin Ahmed, Nour Moustafa, Abu Barkat, Paul Haskell-Dowland

Auditing Information and Cyber Security Governance: A Controls-Based Approach
By Robert E. Davis

Evidence-Based Cybersecurity: Foundations, Research, and Practice
By Pierre-Luc Pomerleau, David Maimon

Operational Auditing: Principles and Techniques for a Changing World
By Hernan Murdock

The Security Leader's Communication Playbook: Bridging the Gap between Security and the Business
By Jeffrey W. Brown

The CISO 3.0: A Guide to Next-Generation Cybersecurity Leadership
By Walt Powell

Securing Talent: Building and Retaining High-Performance Cybersecurity Teams
By Kevin Lynn McLaughlin

For more information about this series please visit: https://www.routledge.com/Security-Audit-and-Leadership-Series/book-series/CRCINTAUDITA?

Securing Talent

Building and Retaining High-Performance Cybersecurity Teams

Kevin Lynn McLaughlin

CRC Press
Taylor & Francis Group
Boca Raton London New York

CRC Press is an imprint of the
Taylor & Francis Group, an **informa** business

Designed cover image: Shutterstock

First edition published 2026
by CRC Press
2385 NW Executive Center Drive, Suite 320, Boca Raton FL 33431

and by CRC Press
4 Park Square, Milton Park, Abingdon, Oxon, OX14 4RN

CRC Press is an imprint of Taylor & Francis Group, LLC

British Library Cataloguing-in-Publication Data
A catalogue record for this book is available from the British Library

ISBN: 978-1-032-61109-9 (hbk)
ISBN: 978-1-032-61114-3 (pbk)
ISBN: 978-1-003-46206-4 (ebk)

DOI: 10.1201/9781003462064

Typeset in Caslon
by SPi Technologies India Pvt Ltd (Straive)

Contents

Acknowledgments

A heartfelt thank you to my family: my wife, Kim, who had been my high school sweetheart and has been my partner for over 40 years, and my three sons, Travis, Kody, and Kory, for their unwavering support and guidance throughout the years.

Special thanks to my dear friend Ibn Akbar for his meticulous editing of this manuscript. His dedication and hard work in refining my ideas and words are deeply valued.

I am grateful to the numerous leaders and mentors I've encountered in my journey. They have been instrumental in shaping my understanding of effective leadership, teaching me both what to do and, equally importantly, what not to do.

Finally, I extend my profound appreciation to Alan Douville, a great friend and mentor. Working alongside him for over a decade has been an honor. Alan, thank you for everything, not least for encouraging this introvert to engage with the world more actively!

Chapter Key Points

Chapter 1

- **Address the Cybersecurity Skills Gap**: The global shortfall of 4.0 million skilled cybersecurity experts highlights a pressing challenge. Factors like rapid tech changes, job stress, and fewer entrants into the field contribute to this gap, leaving organizations at increased risk of cyber threats. This shortage can lead to serious consequences, including data breaches, financial losses, and reputational harm.
- **Build a Retentive Organizational Culture**: Retaining top cybersecurity talent is essential for strong cyber defense. Cultivating an organizational culture that promotes belonging, shared goals, and team commitment is crucial. Key elements include offering continuous learning, encouraging collaboration, providing recognition, ensuring work-life balance, and fostering open communication to keep a motivated and unified team.
- **Foster Industry Collaboration for Cybersecurity Growth**: Tackling the cybersecurity talent shortage requires joint efforts from educational bodies, governments, and the private sector. Developing clear pathways for attracting and retaining cybersecurity talent, coupled with creating team environments

that value their skills, is vital. Such collaborative strategies are necessary to build a strong cybersecurity workforce ready to face sophisticated cyber threats.

Chapter 2

- **Champion Culture as a Leadership Imperative**: The Chief Information Security Officer (CISO) is instrumental in cultivating a positive organizational culture within the cybersecurity team. Through leading with a positive tone and fostering a nurturing environment, the CISO significantly impacts the effectiveness of cybersecurity initiatives. Cultures that value, empower, and offer growth opportunities to employees are key to retaining them and securing their dedication to safeguarding the organization's assets.
- **Encourage Team Collaboration**: Central to an effective cybersecurity culture is a strong emphasis on teamwork and collaborative efforts. The CISO should encourage interactions across different functions, promoting a shared sense of responsibility. This collaborative culture not only enhances outcomes but also fosters a sense of community among team members, boosting team dynamics and efficiency.
- **Set the Standard with Leadership Transparency**: The CISO's commitment to leading by example is crucial. This involves making risk-aware decisions, maintaining transparency, and effective communication. Establishing a culture where accountability and responsibility are clear, coupled with engaging and meaningful work, aligns well with the aspirations of cybersecurity professionals and is essential for their sustained engagement and retention.

Chapter 3

- **Leadership Norms as Team Catalysts**: In cybersecurity, the norms set by leadership, including communication methods, decision-making, and interactions with the team, play a crucial role in shaping team morale and engagement. Positive leadership practices such as open communication, fostering collaboration, and focusing on employee development help create a work environment that supports and values cybersecurity professionals. This kind of environment is key to retaining talent and aligning them with the organization's meaningful mission.

- **Cultivating Team Cohesion through Shared Values**: The collective beliefs, values, and practices within a cybersecurity team, like a dedication to excellence, ongoing learning, ethical conduct, and supportive work dynamics, are essential for the team's effectiveness. These cultural elements encourage strong teamwork and collaborative problem-solving, leading to enhanced performance and results. They also build a more knowledgeable and adaptable team, vital in dealing with the ever-changing cyber threat landscape.
- **Engaging Through Gamification and Continuous Learning**: Implementing gamification in cybersecurity tasks, via activities such as wargames, Capture the Flag (CTF) events, and collaborative exercises, can significantly boost engagement and motivation. Supporting continuous learning through various training methods, including hands-on experiences, formal courses, and self-learning initiatives, is crucial for maintaining an up-to-date and engaged team. This approach not only elevates skills and knowledge but also increases job satisfaction, which is instrumental in achieving higher retention rates.

Chapter 4

- **Integration of Cybersecurity into Organizational Culture**: Successful organizations integrate cybersecurity as a core part of their culture, rather than just a functional necessity. This approach transforms cybersecurity professionals from traditional roles to strategic innovators, deeply involved in the company's growth. Such integration fosters a sense of ownership and purpose among the team, making them feel integral to the organization's success.
- **Emphasis on Continuous Learning and Professional Development**: Organizations leading in cybersecurity culture invest heavily in the continuous learning of their team.

This includes advanced training programs, certification opportunities, attendance at key conferences, and opportunities for cross-functional collaboration. This focus on growth and development helps keep the cybersecurity team ahead of emerging threats and trends, significantly boosting job satisfaction and professional accomplishment.

- **Recognition and Reward System Combined with Innovative Problem-Solving**: Effective cybersecurity cultures employ robust recognition and reward systems, valuing both individual and team contributions. Additionally, diverse and creative problem-solving methodologies, such as the Kepner-Tregoe method and creative brainstorming sessions, are used to tackle challenges. This combined approach of recognizing efforts, encouraging continuous learning, and fostering innovative problem-solving, contributes significantly to creating a dynamic, motivated, and loyal cybersecurity workforce.

Chapter 5

- **Your Leadership Reflects in Your Actions**: It's vital for you, as a cybersecurity leader, to align your actions with your words. Your consistency in practicing the standards and ethics you advocate sets a strong example for your team, building trust and establishing your credibility.
- **Acknowledging Your Team's Efforts is Crucial**: You must recognize and value the contributions of each member of your cybersecurity team. Tailoring your recognition to individual preferences reinforces their sense of worth and appreciation, which in turn boosts morale and enhances team cohesion.
- **Develop Trust Through Mutual Understanding and Feedback**: As a leader, fostering trust with your team is a two-way street. It involves you providing constructive feedback and coaching, especially when addressing mistakes. This approach not only corrects immediate issues but also aids in the professional development and confidence of your team members.

Chapter 6

- **Prioritize Servant Leadership**: Embrace a leadership approach that puts your team's needs and growth at the forefront. By actively supporting their development and creating an environment that empowers them, you foster a sense of value and motivation within the team, crucial for navigating the complexities of cybersecurity.
- **Cultivate a Learning Environment**: Establish a culture where mistakes are viewed as valuable learning opportunities. Encourage open communication and constructive feedback, which not only resolves issues but also strengthens the team's problem-solving abilities and resilience.
- **Emphasize Emotional Intelligence**: Focus on understanding and empathizing with your team's challenges and needs. This emotional awareness is key to creating a supportive atmosphere, essential for maintaining team morale and effectiveness in high-pressure cybersecurity situations.

1

The Foundation of Cybersecurity Success

Culture and Talent Retention

In the field of cybersecurity, securing top talent requires strategic focus, quick decision-making, substantial human interaction, and a measure of creativity. The result, when done correctly, is a splendid and remarkable achievement.

– Dr. Kevin Lynn McLaughlin, PhD

I had recently transitioned from a thriving career in public teaching to what appeared to be a promising new Director level opportunity. On my third day, I left the office at 4 PM to purchase an essential item for our lab from Best Buy. As I arrived there, I received a call from the executive assistant of the organization's top leader. She inquired about my whereabouts. When I explained, she relayed a message from the boss, stating my early departure was totally unacceptable and that I should adhere to the standard office hours of 8:30 AM to 5 PM, like everyone else. Perplexed, I asked about the time for procuring parts and supplies. She bluntly told me that such tasks should be done outside of work hours and never during the time I was expected to be at my desk. That experience from over 30 years ago still resonates with me, evoking feelings of disappointment, anger, guilt, and fear - fear that I had made a terrible mistake in my new career choice. Over the next two years, though, I gained valuable insights, about what not to do as a leader. This book is created with the aim of helping you avoid the pitfalls that lead to difficulties in retaining talent, a lesson underscored from my early career journey.

It is no secret that the cybersecurity profession is faced with a dearth regarding the amount of cybersecurity professionals available. There are far more openings than there are qualified resources to fill them. Projections vary but in general they fall within the general ballparks

DOI: 10.1201/9781003462064-1

discussed in the following sentences. The increasing complexity of cyber threats and the rapid pace of technological advancements have resulted in a demand for skilled cybersecurity professionals that outpaces the current supply. According to the (ISC)^2 Cybersecurity Workforce Study, there is a shortage of 3.4 million cybersecurity professionals worldwide. Note, I recently read an article that said this number has reached 4 million. This shortage of qualified professionals is a significant concern for organizations across industries, as cyber-attacks become more frequent and sophisticated. The absence of sufficient personnel to address these threats leaves organizations vulnerable to data breaches, theft of sensitive information, and reputational damage. The economic impact of these events can be substantial, with the average cost of a data breach estimated to be $3.86 million. The shortage of cybersecurity professionals is further exacerbated by the rapid pace of technological change, which requires a constant effort to stay up to date with the latest trends and techniques. This has resulted in a shortage of trained individuals who possess the right mix of technical, analytical, and interpersonal skills required to effectively address the evolving threat landscape. The cybersecurity field is often viewed as being stressful, challenging and demanding, which can make it difficult to attract and retain qualified professionals. The high stress levels associated with the job, combined with the long hours and intense focus required, can deter individuals who are seeking a more balanced work-life schedule. The shortage of qualified cybersecurity professionals is a pressing concern that requires immediate attention. Organizations must invest in training and development programs to cultivate the next generation of cybersecurity experts, and work to create a positive and rewarding workplace environment to retain top talent. There is currently a significant gap between the number of cybersecurity professionals needed to meet the demand and the number of cybersecurity professionals who are available in the marketplace. This lack is due to diverse number of factors such as lack of investment in cyber security education, limited opportunities for professionals to develop their skills, and an overall shortage of individuals entering the field.

The current lack of qualified cybersecurity professionals is an increasingly pressing concern for organizations who wish to protect their data and assets. *A key hiring theme should be that we will hire smart people who are a good culture fit and keep them.* It is critical that organizations have access to individuals who possess the necessary skills, talent, and knowledge to mitigate these cyber threats. When organizations fall victim to cyber-attacks, they can suffer:

- Data loss or theft: Confidential information such as financial records, personal data, trade secrets, and sensitive company information can be stolen or deleted by the attackers.
- Reputational damage: A successful cyberattack can damage the organization's reputation, causing customers, partners, and investors to lose trust and confidence.
- Financial losses: The cost of responding to the attack, fixing the damage, and paying for any associated lawsuits can result in significant financial losses.
- Business disruption: Operations may be disrupted, causing delays, lost productivity, and lost revenue.
- Legal liability: The organization may be held legally responsible for the data breach and face lawsuits from customers and other affected parties.
- Decreased stock value: A successful cyberattack can also negatively impact the organization's stock price and overall financial performance.
- Loss of intellectual property: Attackers may steal valuable intellectual property, such as proprietary software, research, and development results.
- Compliance violations: Cyberattacks may result in violations of regulations such as data privacy laws, leading to fines and other penalties.

Organizations may have to rely on less qualified individuals to fill the gap in their defenses which could lead to poor cybersecurity programs that are staffed by well-meaning and sometimes energetic and passionate resources who simply lack the skills and expertise to accomplish the task of defending the organization's data and assets.

The shortage of qualified cybersecurity professionals gives rise to a situation where the cost of hiring such professionals has increased dramatically. This puts additional strain on the budgets of many organizations and in many cases, these are unplanned increased expenses. This increase in salaries for cybersecurity professionals causes organizations to compete with one another for the scarce number of cyber security resources with expertise that are available. This makes it difficult for organizations in terms of winning the hiring game through salaries, benefits and other incentives and it makes it even harder to attract the needed expertise in organizations. Many organizations simply do not have the budget capabilities to compete in this highly competitive market space. Organizations such as public-school systems, city and state governments, and nonprofits find it increasingly difficult to hire the experts needed to protect their organizations. The shortage of qualified cybersecurity professionals presents a serious challenge for organizations that are looking to protect their data and assets. With the advent of Artificial Intelligence (AI) and Machine Learning (ML) attack capabilities, along with other sophisticated cyberattack technologies, the cyber threats facing organizations are increasing in both number and difficulty to protect against. This trend makes it imperative that organizations have access to individuals with the necessary skills and knowledge to mitigate these risks and cyberattacks. An issue that confounds this situation is that even when an organization can staff an open position with the right level of cybersecurity expertise the organization's culture is often not capable of retaining the precious resource that they hired. Therefore, instead of becoming the long-term defender the organization needed the cybersecurity expert moves on quickly to an organization who has a culture that resonates with how they expect and want to be treated.

Today's cybersecurity landscape is both complex and interconnected, facing threats from cybercriminals targeting organizations across various sectors. The evolving nature of these threats demands a strong response, yet there's a noticeable shortage of skilled cybersecurity professionals. This gap is largely due to the swift pace of technological changes outpacing the training and educational programs available. Moreover, cybersecurity has often been seen as a niche and challenging field, deterring many potential talents from joining. The impact of this skills shortage is significant. Organizations struggling to find and keep skilled cybersecurity staff are more vulnerable to cyber-attacks. These criminals are constantly finding new ways to breach even the most sophisticated defenses, posing risks not just to individual organizations but to the broader digital ecosystem. To tackle this issue, a joint effort is essential. Educational bodies, government agencies, and private companies must work together to attract, develop, and retain the next wave of cybersecurity experts. This collaborative approach is vital to maintain the resilience and security of our digital world.

The paramount importance of retaining top-tier talent within an organization's cybersecurity team cannot be overstated, and I would argue that the success of a Chief Information Security Officer (CISO) hinges on their ability to attract, cultivate/train, and retain a highly skilled and motivated cadre of cybersecurity professionals. In an age where digital assets are increasingly vulnerable to the attacks of bad actors, a CISO's ability to assemble and retain a formidable team of experts capable of responding to the numerous threats that pervade the wild is not only a strategic priority but also a necessity. An organizational culture that fosters a sense of belonging, shared purpose, and mutual commitment among its members can play a key role in attracting and retaining exceptional talent in the highly competitive field of cybersecurity. The creation and nurturing of such a culture is contingent upon the CISO's ability to instill their team with a sense of mission, a sense of pride, the requisite resources and executive support that enable them to rise to the challenges posed by the increasingly sophistication of cyberattacks. The criticality of keeping top cybersecurity talent for extended periods stems from several factors, not least of which is the complex and highly specialized nature of the field. As cyber threats evolve and proliferate, it is critical for cybersecurity professionals to remain at the vanguard of technological advancements and emerging threat vectors. The cultivation of this expertise requires a substantial investment of time, resources, and energy both on the part of the individual and the organization. Consequently, the loss of such talent can result in a significant reduction of an organization's cyber defense capabilities, leaving it vulnerable to the attacks of cyber enemies.

A high degree of continuity and stability within a cybersecurity team is crucial in fostering the trust, collaboration, and mutual understanding that underpin overall success and highly effective teamwork. As the members of a cybersecurity team navigate the terrain of cyber defense, their ability to work in concert and draw upon their collective expertise is vital to the successful mitigation of threats and the protection of an organization's data and assets. The retention of top talent is therefore integral to the success of a highly functioning and cohesive team, which is in turn crucial to creating and maintaining a robust and resilient cybersecurity posture. Conversely, the loss of highly skilled cybersecurity professionals can have harmful effects on an organization's reputation and ability to attract future talent. In a field where expertise is highly prized, and the competition for top talent is fierce, an organization that is perceived as being unable to retain its most skilled professionals may find itself at a disadvantage when seeking to recruit new talent. The importance of cultivating a strong organizational culture that creates loyalty and a sense of shared commitment among its cybersecurity personnel cannot be overemphasized. *A strong organizational culture, characterized by shared purpose, mutual support, and a commitment to continuous improvement, is indispensable in attracting and retaining the most exceptional talent in the field of cybersecurity.* The success of a CISO and the organization they serve is linked to their ability to assemble, nurture, and retain a highly skilled and motivated team of cybersecurity professionals.

A culture characterized by shared values, a commitment to excellence, and a supportive and inclusive atmosphere is instrumental in attracting and retaining talent in the competitive field of cybersecurity. Such a culture not only enables the cybersecurity team to unite around a common purpose but also empowers and encourages individual team members to hone their skills and obtain satisfaction from their work. Cybersecurity professionals want to know that what they are doing makes a difference in the organization, and in the case of DoD and healthcare/LiveScience organizations a difference for society. Continuous Learning and Professional Development is highly sought by cybersecurity professionals. Therefore, a culture that encourages and facilitates the ongoing professional development of its cybersecurity personnel is well on the way toward retaining talent. This may involve leadership support for attendance at industry conferences, the provision of in-house training opportunities, or the allocation of resources for professional certifications. By nurturing a culture of continuous learning, organizations signal their commitment to the growth and development of their cybersecurity professionals, which in turn can lead to higher loyalty and motivation. An example of this would be a global corporation that invests in a comprehensive professional development program for its cybersecurity team, offering training courses, certifications, and opportunities to attend conferences and workshops. Collaboration and Knowledge Sharing is another item that resonates well among cybersecurity professionals, encouraging a culture of collaboration and knowledge sharing among team members can significantly enhance the cohesion and effectiveness of a cybersecurity team. By fostering an environment where professionals feel comfortable discussing challenges, sharing insights, and getting advice from their peers organizations can promote a sense of camaraderie and mutual support that is critical for increasing retention and motivation. Another example that builds on this team knowledge building and sense of worth would be: a cybersecurity team that regularly conducts collaborative sessions, such as "lunch and learn" or annual/quarterly think tank events, where team members present on relevant topics and engage in discussions to share knowledge and expertise.

Recognition and reward programs in cybersecurity are essential for valuing and acknowledging the significant contributions of your cybersecurity team members. These programs foster motivation and a sense of pride among the team. When cybersecurity leaders implement a system to celebrate outstanding performance, it not only shows appreciation for the hard work and dedication of its staff but also boosts morale and encourages continuous excellence. For instance, consider a financial institution implementing an annual awards program. This program could include several categories of recognition, such as "Cybersecurity Innovator of the Year", "Best Incident Responder", and "Outstanding Team Achievement". These awards would publicly honor the individual or team achievements in various aspects of cybersecurity, acknowledging their vital role in protecting the organization's digital assets. Additionally, these programs can be enriched with more than just accolades. Rewards could include professional development opportunities, such as sponsoring advanced training courses or certifications, invitations to industry conferences, or even leading new high-profile projects. Providing tangible benefits like these not only rewards the current success but also invests in the future growth of the team members. Recognition shouldn't be limited to annual events. Regular acknowledgments, such as shout-outs in company meetings or newsletters, help maintain a consistent level of engagement and appreciation. Maintaining high morale and making sure team members feel valued year-round is crucial. Effective reward and recognition programs in cybersecurity need to be comprehensive, incorporating both visible acknowledgment and substantial benefits. This demonstrates the organization's appreciation and commitment to its cybersecurity staff, fostering a culture that values both individual achievements and a continuous pursuit of excellence. Recognizing that each individual values different forms of acknowledgment, a skilled cybersecurity leader takes the time to understand what type of recognition resonates most with each team member. They tailor rewards and acknowledgments to align with those preferences, ensuring the recognition is meaningful and within the individual's comfort zone.

It's important to move away from outdated expectations like assuming cybersecurity professionals should routinely work extended hours, weekends, or through holidays as part of their job. Such a mindset needs immediate revision. The reality is, while many in the field might choose to work long hours, this should never be a default expectation or a factor in determining rewards and recognition. In the ever-evolving and high-pressure domain of cybersecurity, prioritizing and cultivating a healthy work-life balance is more than just a luxury; it's a necessity. To ensure that your team members remain motivated and invested in their roles, emphasize the importance of flexible work arrangements. These not only cater to different lifestyles but also acknowledge that a one-size-fits-all approach isn't effective. Encouraging team members to strive for balance better equips them to manage the stress and demanding hours associated with handling Cyber Incident Response Team (CIRT) levels of incidents. Methods like taking regular breaks, whether for gratitude walks or simple pauses, can significantly reduce burnout and rejuvenate the mind, ultimately improving focus and performance during critical incidents. By introducing dedicated "think" and "exploration" times, companies provide team members with opportunities to brainstorm, innovate, and stay updated with the latest industry trends. A forward-thinking tech company, for instance, might empower its cybersecurity team with flexible hours or remote work options, enabling them to maintain a balance between professional duties and personal commitments.

Such practices not only foster greater job satisfaction and reduce the risk of burnout but also strengthen overall team efficiency, resilience, and long-term effectiveness.

Openness and Transparency is crucial in fostering trust and confidence among cybersecurity teams. By maintaining an ongoing dialogue with team members, soliciting their input, and keeping them informed of the organization's strategic objectives and challenges, leaders can create an atmosphere of inclusion and mutual respect that is conducive to retention and motivation. An example of this would be a healthcare organization whose CISO regularly holds town hall meetings with the cybersecurity team, providing updates on the organization's security posture and inviting feedback and suggestions from team members. In essence a strong organizational culture that embodies norms such as *continuous learning, collaboration, recognition, work-life balance, and open communication* is vital in impacting the retention and motivation of cybersecurity professionals. By cultivating such a culture, organizations can significantly enhance the appeal and longevity of their cybersecurity workforce, ensuring the continued resilience and security of their digital assets in the face of an increasingly hostile cyber threat landscape. We will talk in more detail on these items in later chapters.

In the cybersecurity profession, cultivating a positive and supportive work culture is key to building and retaining top-tier teams. Inspired by leadership experts like Ken Blanchard, John P. Strelecky, Steve Farber, and Tom Rath, it's clear that a workplace rooted in optimism, shared values, and a nurturing atmosphere significantly boosts team success. This positive culture not only allows individuals to develop their skills and find satisfaction in their work but also fosters a strong sense of unity and shared commitment within the team. A vital element in creating such a culture is establishing a clear vision and purpose. When team members understand their role in achieving the organization's goals, they're more likely to feel a deep sense of meaning and connection to their work, fostering loyalty to the team and the wider organization. Additionally, promoting personal and professional growth is essential in retaining skilled cybersecurity professionals. By offering continuous learning and career development opportunities, organizations can show their commitment to their employees' well-being and success, leading to higher job satisfaction and motivation. Empowering employees by delegating responsibility, encouraging autonomy, and maintaining open communication is another crucial aspect of a positive workplace. Such an environment enables individuals to feel valued and take ownership of their work, enhancing engagement and the effectiveness of the cybersecurity team. Recognizing and leveraging the unique strengths of each team member, as highlighted by Rath, is also important. *A strengths-based approach encourages individuals to excel in their natural talents, boosting confidence, productivity, and retention.* Moreover, fostering an inclusive culture where everyone feels a strong sense of belonging and support, particularly during challenging times, is crucial for maintaining team cohesion.

The critical nature of the cybersecurity talent shortage is evident. The combination of rising cyber threats, technological progression, and a limited number of skilled professionals poses a significant challenge. It's not just about filling vacancies but retaining professionals who align with the organization's culture and mission. As cybersecurity becomes increasingly vital to business and societal stability, addressing this talent gap is crucial. This requires a concerted effort from industry leaders, educational bodies, and policymakers to develop strategies for attracting and retaining the cybersecurity experts of the future. Creating supportive team environments that respect and value these professionals is equally important for organizations to effectively navigate the complexities of the cyber world.

Chapter 1 Notable Passages and key points

- *"In a field where expertise is highly prized, and the competition for top talent is fierce, an organization that is perceived as being unable to retain its most skilled professionals may find itself at a disadvantage when seeking to recruit new talent."*
- *"A strong organizational culture, characterized by shared purpose, mutual support, and a commitment to continuous improvement, is indispensable in attracting and retaining the most exceptional talent in the field of cybersecurity."*
  - Culture drives retention and success in cybersecurity.
  - Leadership that inspires trust and growth builds strong teams.
  - Losing talent weakens defenses and disrupts continuity.

2

Leadership in Action

Setting the Cybersecurity Culture from the Top

The Tone from the Top is paramount in crafting a formidable cyber culture. The CISO's role in fostering a strong and united team is instrumental to the overall success of an organization's cybersecurity posture.

– Dr. Kevin Lynn McLaughlin, PhD

Setting the Foundation for a Strong Culture is a crucial concept for any organization, particularly when it comes to the field of cybersecurity. The role of the CISO in establishing and nurturing a strong culture within the cybersecurity team cannot be overstated. A CISO who takes a leadership position in setting the tone from the top and creating a positive culture has tremendous positive effect on the success of their organization's cybersecurity efforts. A dedicated focus on employee retention begins with the recognition that employees are a critical component of any successful cybersecurity program. *A positive culture that values and empowers employees, provides opportunities for growth and development, and recognizes the key role that everyone plays in protecting the organization's assets is essential for retaining employees and ensuring their continued commitment to the organization.* The CISO plays a critical role in establishing and nurturing this positive culture. Leading by example and walking the talk is essential for creating a culture where employees feel valued and respected. Having a simple mission statement for the cybersecurity team members such as, we protect the organization's data and assets, is critical to ensuring that all the cybersecurity team members not only understand their primary role, but they also understand and become invested in waking up every day knowing they are of value to the organization's success or failure. By setting the tone from the top

DOI: 10.1201/9781003462064-2

and showing the importance of cybersecurity, the CISO can help to create a culture where employees are proud to work for the organization and feel valued for their contributions. The CISO should also communicate the importance of cybersecurity knowledge to all their cybersecurity team members and provide them with the training and resources they need to understand their role in protecting the organization's assets. This will help to ensure that the team is knowledgeable about the organization's cybersecurity policies and procedures and feel empowered to carry out their responsibilities effectively.

Another key aspect of creating a positive culture is the promotion of collaboration and teamwork. The CISO should encourage cross-functional collaboration to ensure that everyone is working together toward a common goal. This will help to foster a sense of community and shared responsibility, which is critical in building a strong culture of cybersecurity. I cannot stress enough the importance of promoting collaboration and teamwork in building a strong culture within the cybersecurity and broader organizational teams. A strong culture is not just about having the right policies and procedures in place, but also about having a team that works well together and feels a sense of shared responsibility for their work. Encouraging cross-functional collaboration is one of the most effective ways to build a sense of community and shared responsibility among not just cybersecurity team members but also with other department's team members. When team members from different functions work together on a project or task, they get to know each other better, understand each other's strengths and weaknesses, and learn how to work together more effectively. This not only leads to better outcomes but also helps to foster a sense of community and shared responsibility. You can encourage cross-functional collaboration by setting up regular cross-functional team meetings, assigning team members to work on projects together, and actively seeking out opportunities for cross-functional collaboration. Furthermore, inviting strategic external team members to annual cybersecurity team leadership and strategy meetings can further integrate these efforts, ensuring alignment and shared vision. Additionally, recognizing the contributions of key partners by inviting the best-performing partner to attend a cybersecurity conference with cybersecurity team members can enhance mutual understanding and strengthen partnerships. Finally, creating a positive team culture by recognizing and rewarding team members for working well together and promoting a sense of shared responsibility reinforces these collaborative initiatives.

Creating a strong culture requires the CISO to lead by example and walk their talk. When a CISO is "walking their talk", they are demonstrating the values, behaviors, and attitudes they expect from their team members. They are not just talking about culture, cybersecurity and risk management but living it out in their own actions and decisions. This sends a powerful message to the team and sets the tone for an effective team culture. For example, if a CISO wants their team to prioritize a risk focus in their work, they need to demonstrate this themselves by consistently making decisions based on risk a priority in their own work and decisions. If they want their team to be transparent and communicate effectively, they need to model this behavior by being open and transparent in their own communications. For a CISO walking their talk means aligning one's actions with one's words and consistently demonstrating the behaviors and values you expect from others. When you do this, it builds trust, respect, and credibility among cybersecurity team members and sets a positive example for the entire organization. Further, it provides a sense of consistency and integrity that cybersecurity professionals appreciate and are looking for when they make their long-term decisions to stay on a team or go work someplace else.

Setting the tone at the top that can be used to motivate and engage the cybersecurity team is important. One of these messages must be on the importance of cybersecurity in all areas of the organization. The CISO should communicate the importance of cybersecurity to the cybersecurity team members and provide them with the training and resources they need to understand their role in protecting the organization's assets. This approach and methodology provide the team members with a strong feeling of value and self-worth. In addition to communicating the importance of cybersecurity, the CISO must also create a culture of accountability and responsibility. This means creating a clear set of policies, processes and procedures that outline how tasks are performed and completed. The creation of Standard Operating procedures (SOPs) and the added creation of runbooks for the various towers, such as Red Team, Threat Hunting,

SecOps, Cybersecurity Automation, Threat Intelligence, etc. provides a foundational set of instructions that takes ambiguity out of known and repeatable tasks. This can provide a sense of confidence that simple tasks can be completed quickly, and the team members' time can be focused and better spent on the harder items which require their higher-level thinking skills. Providing processes and procedures that allow for team members to focus on the more engaging and interesting work resonates well with the mind set and interests of most cybersecurity professionals. Having runbooks available also allows new team members to get up to speed and trained quickly and efficiently.

A CISO who takes a leadership role in creating a positive culture and setting the tone from the top will have a significant impact on the success of their organization's cybersecurity personnel retention efforts. *Additionally, a CISO who takes a leadership role in creating a positive culture can have a tremendous impact on the overall success on the continuity of the cybersecurity team.* A positive culture is not just about having a happy and motivated team, but having a team that is more driven, motivated, productive, engaged, and committed to the organization's goals. A positive culture starts with leadership, by taking a proactive approach to creating a positive culture, CISOs not only build a more engaged and motivated team, but also create a more positive and productive work environment. A positive and engaging work environment significantly improves the retention of cybersecurity team members. One of the key concepts in creating a positive culture is to focus on the positive and to promote positivity and energy in the workplace. This idea is well-described in books such as "How Full is Your Bucket?" by Tom Rath and Donald Clifton and "The Energy Bus" by Jon Gordon. These books, which are a mandatory read for any new team member who joins a team I am leading, emphasize the importance of focusing on the positive and promoting positivity in the workplace to build a more engaged and motivated team. As the CISO, you take the leadership role in promoting positivity by focusing on what is working well, recognizing, and rewarding team members for their positive contributions, and fostering a positive, psychologically safe, and supportive work environment. Additionally, you can build on that positive culture by promoting open communication, encouraging teamwork and collaboration, and creating opportunities for team members to connect and build relationships with one another. A positive culture starts with leadership, and as the CISO, you play a critical role in shaping the culture of the cybersecurity team. By taking an approach of positivity in building your culture, you build a more engaged and motivated team, create a more positive and productive work environment, and drive better team outcomes and team retention. When you focus on leading by example, walking the talk, and promoting collaboration and teamwork, you build a strong and resilient culture that can protect the organization's assets against cyber threats.

When I say that we lead through positivity, I am not suggesting that we ignore problems or avoid addressing mistakes. On the contrary, leading through positivity means that we approach challenges and mistakes with a positive and constructive mindset. We take the time to understand what went wrong, we identify opportunities for improvement, and we work together to find a solution. It is also important to note that leading through positivity does not mean being friendly at the cost of holding team members accountable. We are all responsible for maintaining the highest level of cybersecurity and ethics in all that we do, and when mistakes are made, it is our responsibility to address them. But we do so in a way that is respectful, supportive, and focused on learning and growth. Leading through positivity does not mean pretending that bad things do not happen. We all make mistakes, and that is okay. What is important is how we respond to those mistakes. Do we yell and scream and pout at each other, or do we approach the situation with a positive and constructive mindset? By leading through positivity, we demonstrate to each other and to those around us that we are a team that is focused on growth, improvement, and success. So, let us continue to lead through positivity and embrace the challenges and opportunities that come our way. Let us support each other, learn from our mistakes, and drive on to be better. Together, we can make a positive impact.

I have seen the importance of trust and transparency firsthand in the corporate world. It is a well-known fact that the tone set by leaders has a ripple effect throughout an organization, and it is no different in the realm of cybersecurity. A CISO who takes a leadership role in creating a culture of trust and transparency sends a clear message to their team that they value open communication and honesty. When team members feel that their contributions are valued and their concerns are heard, they are more likely to feel a sense of loyalty to the organization and a commitment to the success of the team. This type of culture also allows for an open and honest exchange of ideas, which is essential for the growth and development of the team. In my experience, it is also important for the CISO to lead by example in this regard. If they are transparent and honest in their own interactions with team members, they are much more likely to foster a culture of trust throughout the organization. This, in turn, will encourage team members to feel comfortable sharing their own ideas and concerns, leading to a more collaborative and productive work environment. One of the key elements of creating a culture of trust and transparency is to provide ongoing opportunities for team members to connect and build relationships. This could be in the form of regular team-building activities, open forums, or simply taking the time to have informal conversations with team members. The more opportunities team members have to connect with one another, the stronger the sense of community and shared responsibility will become. *Building a culture of trust and transparency is critical for the success of any cybersecurity team, and it starts with the CISO setting the right tone from the top.* By creating opportunities for team members to connect, valuing open communication and honesty, and leading by example, the CISO can help build a team that is productive, innovative, and committed to success.

The other item that will help high performing teams and their leaders maintain high retention and a fun and rewarding work environment is through the promoting of diversity and inclusion. Diversity and inclusion play a significant role in fostering trust and transparency as well as a diversity of great ideas within your cybersecurity team. Diversity and inclusion mean creating a workplace where everyone feels valued and respected, regardless of their race, ethnicity, gender, age, religion, sexual orientation, or any other characteristic that makes them unique. When we promote diversity and inclusion, we are sending a message that everyone is welcome, and that everyone has something valuable to contribute. This kind of inclusive environment fosters trust and transparency in several ways. Firstly, when people feel valued and respected, they are more likely to be open and honest in their interactions with others. This leads to better communication and collaboration, which is essential for success in the cybersecurity field. Secondly, promoting diversity and inclusion helps to break down barriers and promotes understanding between team members. When people come from diverse backgrounds and have different perspectives, they bring innovative ideas and approaches to problem-solving. This can lead to more innovative solutions and a better understanding of the challenges we face. Thirdly, promoting diversity and inclusion helps to create a more inclusive workplace culture, where everyone feels comfortable and confident in their abilities. This leads to a more positive and productive work environment, which in turn can lead to better results and a stronger, more cohesive team. Promoting diversity and inclusion is one of the essential components for creating a workplace where trust and transparency are the norm. By fostering an inclusive environment, we can break down barriers, promote understanding, and create a more positive and productive workplace culture.

The role of a CISO in shaping and nurturing a positive cybersecurity culture cannot be overstated. By setting the tone from the top, the CISO serves as both a guide and a role model, demonstrating the values, behaviors, and attitudes necessary for a thriving cybersecurity team. Leadership by example, walking the talk, creates a foundation of trust, transparency, and accountability, all of which are essential to retaining talent and fostering an environment where team members feel valued and empowered. Encouraging collaboration and teamwork across both internal and external stakeholders is equally important. By involving diverse perspectives, promoting shared responsibility, and inviting strategic partners to leadership and strategy meetings or conferences, organizations strengthen relationships and align goals. This builds not only a cohesive cybersecurity team but also a broader culture of unity and purpose. At the core of a strong cybersecurity culture is positivity. Addressing challenges constructively, learning from mistakes, and celebrating both individual and team achievements cultivate an atmosphere of growth and motivation. This is complemented by a commitment to diversity and inclusion, ensuring all voices are valued and respected. Such an environment fosters innovation and adaptability, critical for navigating the ever-evolving cyber threat landscape. Focusing on collaboration, recognition, inclusivity, and continuous learning, CISOs can lead their teams to greater effectiveness and resilience. A strong and positive culture is not just a tool for retention, it is a strategic advantage that enhances the organization's overall cybersecurity posture. Ultimately, this approach ensures that teams are not only prepared to meet today's challenges but are equipped to thrive in the face of future threats.

Chapter 2 Notable Passages and key points

- *"Promoting diversity and inclusion means creating a workplace where everyone feels valued and respected, regardless of their unique characteristics. This kind of inclusive environment not only fosters trust and transparency but also invites a wealth of innovative ideas within the cybersecurity team."*
- *"Leading through positivity does not mean pretending that bad things do not happen… What is important is how we respond to those mistakes.*
  - The tone set by leadership defines the culture and success of the cybersecurity team.
  - Trust, transparency, and inclusion are foundational to building a cohesive and resilient team.
  - Positive leadership inspires collaboration, accountability, and retention in the face of cyber challenges.

3

Leadership Shadow

Shaping Cybersecurity Culture Through Norms and Values

Effective leadership norms and a positive leadership culture create an enjoyable and high energy atmosphere for cybersecurity team members which helps prevent talent loss.

– Dr. Kevin Lynn McLaughlin, PhD

Leadership norms and cultural items are critical components that play a significant role in motivating cybersecurity professionals and maintaining high retention rates. These norms refer to the established practices, beliefs, and values within a cybersecurity team that shape the behavior of its team members. Leadership norms can have a significant impact on the morale and engagement of cybersecurity professionals, and it is essential for cybersecurity leaders to plan, identify and understand them to effectively motivate and retain talent. *Leadership norms refer to the standards of behavior and expectations set by cybersecurity leaders for the team.* Leadership norms can include things like communication styles, decision-making processes, and the ways in which the leaders interact with team members. When cybersecurity leaders exhibit positive leadership norms, such as open communication, collaboration, and a focus on employee development, it can create a positive and supportive work environment that is more likely to retain cybersecurity professionals. A cybersecurity leader's communication style refers to the way in which they communicate with their team members. This can include things like the tone of voice, the level of detail provided in communication, setting a positive tone; even when talking about a mistake and learning from it, as well as the frequency of communication. Decision-making processes are an important aspect of cybersecurity leadership norms, decision-making processes

DOI: 10.1201/9781003462064-3

refer to the ways in which leaders make decisions and involve their employees in the process. Some examples of ways to positively involve cybersecurity team members in the decision-making process are:

- Encourage open communication: Leaders can create an environment where employees feel comfortable providing input and sharing their opinions. This can be achieved through regular one-on-one meetings, team meetings, or open forums where employees can share their thoughts and ideas.
- Seek input from multiple perspectives: Cybersecurity Leaders can gather input from different departments and levels within the organization to get a comprehensive understanding of the issue at hand. This can help to ensure that decisions are well-informed and consider the perspectives of all stakeholders.
- Hold team brainstorming sessions: Cybersecurity Leaders can bring their team together to brainstorm and produce solutions to a particular issue. This can help to generate innovative ideas and encourage employees to think creatively.
- Encourage participation in decision-making committees: Leaders can form committees composed of employees from different departments to make decisions on specific topics. This can help to ensure that the perspectives of all stakeholders are considered, and alignment is gained.
- Involve employees in pilot programs: Leaders can involve employees in pilot programs or experiments to test latest ideas and gather feedback. This can provide employees with a sense of ownership and help to ensure that decisions are based on practical experience.

Cultural items refer to the shared beliefs, values, and practices that are held by the talent on a cybersecurity team. Some of the best-in-class shared beliefs for a high performing and highly engaged cybersecurity team include:

- A commitment to excellence: The team should believe in always striving for excellence in their work and be willing to put in the effort required to achieve the best possible results.
- A focus on continuous learning: The team should have a shared belief in the importance of continuous learning and

should be committed to staying up to date with the latest developments and trends in the field. Note—the cost burden of the training should not be on the employee who is gaining the knowledge needed to protect the organization better.

- A strong sense of teamwork: The team should believe in the power of collaboration and should work together as a cohesive unit to achieve common goals.
- A commitment to ethical behavior: The team should believe in acting with integrity and following a strict code of conduct, which can help to build trust and credibility both within the team and with stakeholders.
- A focus on results: The team should be results-oriented and should be committed to delivering high-quality work that meets the needs of the organization.
- A supportive and inclusive work environment: The team should believe in creating a work environment that is supportive and inclusive, where team members feel valued and respected, regardless of their background or experience.
- Recognition and rewards for outstanding performance: The team should believe in recognizing and rewarding team members for their outstanding performance, which can help to motivate and inspire them to do their best work.

Research data clearly indicates that cultural values play a significant role in the success and retention of a cybersecurity team. An intense sense of teamwork fosters a sense of camaraderie and collaboration within the team, leading to more efficient problem-solving and better results. *Continuous learning is a crucial aspect of any cybersecurity team*. In today's rapidly evolving cyberattack landscape, it is imperative for team members to stay current with the latest developments and trends to effectively protect their organization's assets. A focus on continuous learning can lead to a more knowledgeable and adaptable team, making them better equipped to handle the challenges that come their way.

The use of gamification can also be an effective tool in encouraging retention of cybersecurity professionals. By incorporating game-like elements into the work environment, which provides competition and rewards, cybersecurity teams can make the work more engaging and enjoyable for team members, leading to higher levels of motivation and satisfaction. There are several activities that cybersecurity teams can engage in to leverage the strengths of gamification, including:

- Wargames: These are simulated cyberattack scenarios that test the skills and knowledge of the cybersecurity team. By participating in wargames, team members can hone their skills and improve their ability to respond to real-world threats.
- Capture the Flag (CTF) events: CTF events are competitive challenges that test the cybersecurity skills of participants. They often involve solving puzzles, cracking codes, and finding vulnerabilities in simulated systems. Participating in CTF events can help to build teamwork, as well as provide opportunities for continuous learning and growth.
- Red Team vs Blue Team exercises: In these exercises, one team acts as the "red team," simulating an attacker, while the other team acts as the "blue team," defending the simulated system. These exercises can help to build collaboration and communication within the cybersecurity team, as well as provide opportunities for continuous learning and improvement.
- Cybersecurity challenges and competitions: These events bring together cybersecurity professionals from around the world to compete and display their skills. By participating in these challenges, team members can gain exposure to modern technologies, techniques, and methodologies, and build relationships with other professionals in the field.
- Traditional gaming events: The use of traditional games to help team members bond should not be overlooked. Organizing gaming events, such as video game tournaments or board game nights (they now have cybersecuirty board games), can provide opportunities for team members to bond and have fun together. Consider online activities such as Kahoot to foster bonding and getting to know each other. By creating a positive and enjoyable work environment, organizations can help to foster a sense of camaraderie and build stronger relationships within the team. (add something about ninja awards, or karate ranks, star pilot titles, etc.)

As mentioned previously in this chapter, continuous learning is important to cybersecurity professionals. The role of the cyber-defender is a difficult one and the bad actors are continuously training to have an edge in the cyber arena; without being able to keep their skills current your cybersecurity team members will become disengaged and start looking elsewhere, usually outside your company, to get the skills, they feel they need to be successful. Providing robust cybersecurity training and learning opportunities is vital for the success and retention of a high-performing and highly engaged cybersecurity team. To provide the best-in-class methods for these opportunities, organizations should consider a combination of on-the-job training, formal classroom training, attending conferences and workshops, self-directed learning, and gamification. On-the-job training provides team members with hands-on experience and allows them to develop their skills in real-world scenarios. This can be done through mentorship programs, shadowing experienced team members, or working on real-world projects. Formal classroom training, on the other hand, provides structured learning opportunities, where team members can gain knowledge and skills in a controlled environment, such as in-person training sessions, online courses, and certification programs. Attending conferences and workshops can provide team members with the opportunity to network with other professionals in the field, learn about the latest developments and trends, and gain exposure to new technologies and methodologies. Self-directed learning, where team members take ownership of their own learning and development, can also be highly effective. As previously stated, gamification can make the learning process more enjoyable and engaging for team members by incorporating game-like elements, such as simulations, challenges, and competitions to test and improve skills, or using gamification to motivate and encourage continuous learning. *Providing robust cybersecurity training and learning opportunities is essential for the success and retention of a high-performing and highly engaged cybersecurity team.* By combining on-the-job training, formal classroom training, attending conferences and workshops, self-directed learning, gamification, and cost-effective online training solutions such as Linked-In Learning or Pluralsight, organizations can help to support and motivate their cybersecurity team, leading to better results and higher levels of employee satisfaction. Some examples of lower cost trainings and learning opportunities are:

- Online courses: There are many online courses available that provide in-depth training on a variety of cybersecurity topics. These courses are often cost effective and can be completed at the team member's own pace and often come with certification options.
- Webinars: Webinars are online seminars that can provide team members with an opportunity to learn about specific topics from experts in the field. They are often interactive and provide opportunities for team members to ask questions and engage with the presenter.
- Open-source tools and resources: There are many open-source tools and resources available that can help team members to learn about specific topics and improve their skills. This can include online tutorials, documentation, and forums where team members can connect with others in the field.
- Zero or minimal cost conferences are often available in many of the major cities across the globe.

Each cybersecurity leader needs to sit down and think about what their vision is for the team culture they want to foster and be a leader of. Keep in mond that culture needs to be intentional. Some of the main cultural themes that resonate with me and that I like to make use of these will be discussed in much more detail in subsequent chapters, are based on books such as "How Full is Your Bucket", "The Energy Bus", "The Sale", "The Monk and the Ferrari" and the "Why Café". Taking portions of the leadership cultures from these books and mixing them with items such as the Senn Delaney Culture trainings makes for a very powerful foundation for building a high performing, highly engaged cybersecurity team. By taking portions of the leadership cultures from these books and incorporating them with items such as the Senn Delaney or Gallup Culture trainings, organizations can build an immensely powerful foundation for a high-performing, highly engaged cybersecurity team. For example, the book "How Full is Your Bucket" focuses on the importance of positivity and the impact that it can have on an individual's overall well-being and success. By promoting a positive work environment, organizations can help to build a more motivated and engaged team, which can lead to better results. Similarly, "The Energy Bus" emphasizes the importance of maintaining a positive attitude and focus on the future, even in the face of challenges and setbacks. By fostering a sense of optimism and resilience within the team, organizations can help team members to stay motivated and focused, even in the face of adversity. "The Sale" is another book that can provide valuable insights into building a high-performing, highly engaged team. This book focuses on the importance of relationships and communication, and how they can impact success. By promoting a culture of open communication and collaboration, organizations can help to build stronger relationships within the team, leading to better results. In addition, "The Monk and the Ferrari" emphasizes the importance of balance and finding purpose in one's work. By providing team members with a sense of purpose and direction, organizations can help to keep them motivated and engaged and ensure that they are able to achieve their full potential. Finally, "The Why Café" focuses on the importance of creating a work environment that supports and motivates team members. The book explores the idea that *people are more engaged and motivated when they understand the purpose behind their work, and that organizations that create a culture of purpose are more likely to be successful.* It provides practical guidance on how organizations can create a work environment that supports and motivates team members, and how individuals can find meaning and purpose in their work. The opinion espoused in the "Why Café" is that by creating a work environment where people feel that their work has purpose and meaning, organizations can foster greater engagement, motivation, and success. These books when combined with leveraging the methodologies presented in the book "Winning Teams, Winning Cultures" by Larry Senn and Jim Hart, provide a solid foundation for creating your high performing, highly retained cybersecurity team. "Winning Teams, Winning cultures" talks about items such as: "The Shadow of the Leader" which can provide valuable insights into how organizations can create a high-performing and highly engaged team. Another one of the key cultural ideas presented in the book is the concept of "Be here now". This involves encouraging team members to focus on the present moment and to be fully engaged in their work. By promoting a sense of mindfulness and presence, organizations can help to reduce stress and improve performance, leading to better results. A disruptor that I cause when coming on a new team is to put a ban on laptops at meetings, which is just a form of don't do email be present in the meeting. Yes, of course, I will allow team members to take notes on their tablet or your laptop if they are truly wanting to do that. Even then there is a zero-tolerance policy on multi-tasking just because they have their laptop or tablet with them. As another form of helping ensure a be here now attitude and behavior I limit the amount of my team members who attend non-department meetings to the one, two if absolutely necessary, people who are critical to the meeting's success. Another cultural idea presented in the "Winning Teams, Winning Culture" book is the "Mood Elevator". This involves creating a work environment that supports and motivates team members and helps to keep them in a positive state of mind. This can involve promoting a positive work culture, providing opportunities for team members to engage in activities that they enjoy, and encouraging team members to focus on their strengths and accomplishments. The use of the mood elevator also helps team members make conscious decisions if they should engage at a time when they are low on the mood elevator, as that type of engagement is usually very nonproductive and is almost always destructive to the overall team atmosphere. The importance of feedback and how it can be used to improve performance is also discussed in "Winning Teams Winning Cultures". By providing regular and constructive feedback, cybersecurity leaders can help team members to understand their strengths and weaknesses, and to identify areas for improvement. The proper use of feedback can lead to greater engagement, motivation, and better results.

It is important to understand that as a leader you are uniquely positioned to drive the success of the cybersecurity team and more importantly to drive the atmosphere and behaviors that make up the team's work environment. The shadow you cast in your role as a leader for the team is one that cannot be overstated. The team adjusts and imitates the behaviors you show when you are interacting within the team and external to the team. By promoting a positive and supportive leadership style, you build a high-performing and highly engaged team. This does involve encouraging leaders to be approachable, to provide regular feedback, and to create a work environment that supports and motivates team members.

Leadership norms and cultural values are the bedrock upon which successful and enduring cybersecurity teams are built. These elements, though often intangible, play a critical role in shaping the behavior, motivation, and engagement of team members. In this chapter, we explored how leadership norms, those standards of behavior and expectations set by cybersecurity leaders, create the atmosphere in which teams operate. When leaders demonstrate positive norms, such as open communication, inclusive decision-making, collaboration, and a focus on employee development, they establish a foundation that fosters trust, morale, and a sense of shared purpose. The chapter highlighted the importance of deliberate and thoughtful leadership. A cybersecurity leader's shadow—the attitudes, behaviors, and decisions they project—significantly influences the team's dynamics. Leaders who are approachable, transparent, and supportive inspire their teams to mirror those values, cultivating a culture of positivity and mutual respect. We discussed practical methods leaders can use to enhance team cohesion, including collaborative decision-making processes, fostering a sense of ownership among team members, and integrating gamification into both training and daily work. Activities such as Capture the Flag (CTF) events, wargames, and team challenges not only enhance technical skills but also make work more engaging and enjoyable, leading to higher retention rates. Cultural values were another key focus. These shared beliefs and practices—ranging from a commitment to excellence and continuous learning to fostering an inclusive and supportive work environment—are crucial in aligning the team with the organization's goals. *Teams that prioritize ethical behavior, value teamwork, and celebrate individual and collective achievements are more likely to excel.* Providing robust training opportunities, whether through on-the-job mentorship, formal education, or online resources, ensures that team members remain engaged and equipped to handle evolving threats.

Additionally, we examined the concept of positivity as a driving force behind team culture. Drawing inspiration from works such as *How Full is Your Bucket?* and *The Energy Bus*, we explored how fostering a positive and resilient mindset enables teams to navigate challenges with greater confidence and effectiveness. Leadership, we noted, is not just about solving problems but about setting the tone for how those problems are approached, with a constructive and forward-thinking attitude. Finally, we reinforced the idea that creating a high-performing cybersecurity team goes beyond technical prowess; it requires a deep understanding of human dynamics. Leaders who actively promote open communication, continuous learning, and a supportive environment will find that their teams are more innovative, collaborative, and committed to the organization's mission. A culture shaped by positive leadership norms and shared values is not only a safeguard against talent loss but a strategic advantage in the ever-evolving cybersecurity landscape. As a cybersecurity leader, your actions, decisions, and mindset echo throughout your team. By cultivating a strong culture based on well-defined leadership norms and shared values, you are not only protecting your organization's digital assets but also empowering your team to reach its highest potential.

Chapter 3 Notable Passages and key points

- *"When cybersecurity leaders exhibit positive leadership norms, such as open communication, collaboration, and a focus on employee development, they can create a positive work environment that supports and motivates team members."*
- *"By promoting a culture of open communication, cybersecurity leaders can help to build stronger relationships within the team and ensure that team members are able to work together effectively. This can lead to improved collaboration and better results."*
    - Leadership norms set the tone for a motivated and engaged cybersecurity team.
    - A culture of open communication, collaboration, and continuous learning drives team success.
    - The leader's shadow shapes the team's behavior, morale, and retention.

4

Elevating Cybersecurity Culture and Retention

Investing in cybersecurity talent retention is not merely an operational tactic; it's a holistic methodology. Putting together strategies that value the expertise and strengths of each team member, creates an environment that is resistant to both talent loss and cyber threats.

– Kevin L. McLaughlin, PhD

In an era where data breaches and cyberattacks are an ever-present threat, cultivating a robust cybersecurity culture has become critical for organizations across the globe. The creation of this culture goes far beyond implementing cybersecurity protocols and controls; it passes through every part of an organization, instilling a sense of collective responsibility toward the protection of data and assets. This chapter talks about the journey of several fictional organizations that have successfully woven a strong cybersecurity culture into their operational environment, not only safeguarding themselves from cyber threats but also retaining their cybersecurity talent well beyond industry averages.

At Organization A, cybersecurity is not just a function; it is a vital part of the company's culture and a key contributor to its success. This philosophy sets Organization A apart as a leader in creating an exemplary cybersecurity workplace. They understand that a robust focus on cybersecurity not only protects the company but also retains and motivates top talent. In this environment, cybersecurity professionals are not confined to traditional roles of safeguarding digital assets. They are encouraged to contribute creatively to the company's growth, transforming them from mere defenders into innovators and strategic assets. This approach has nurtured a sense of ownership and integration among the cybersecurity team. They do not just see themselves as operatives working in isolation to fend off cyber threats. Instead, they

DOI: 10.1201/9781003462064-4

view themselves as integral components of the organization, directly influencing its direction and success. This integration is a deliberate outcome of the leadership's vision at Organization A, where cybersecurity is seen as a collective responsibility, vital to every aspect of the organization. The leadership's commitment to fostering a learning and growth-centric environment further distinguishes Organization A. This commitment to fostering professional growth is evident in several key areas:

1. **Advanced Training Programs**: Organization A invests in advanced training programs that cover the latest trends and technologies in cybersecurity. These programs are designed to keep their professionals ahead of the curve, equipping them with the knowledge and skills to tackle emerging threats and vulnerabilities.
2. **Certification Opportunities**: The company supports and finances certification courses for its cybersecurity team. This includes industry-recognized certifications like CISSP, CISM, and CEH, which are crucial for career advancement and staying current in the field.
3. **Conferences and Workshops**: Cybersecurity professionals at Organization A are encouraged to attend leading conferences and workshops. This not only provides them with networking opportunities but also exposes them to innovative ideas, trends, and best practices in cybersecurity.
4. **Cross-Functional Collaboration**: The organization promotes cross-functional collaboration, allowing cybersecurity professionals to work alongside other departments such as IT, legal, and operations. This broadens their understanding of the business as a whole and how cybersecurity integrates and supports various facets of the company.
5. **Mentorship Programs**: Experienced cybersecurity leaders within the organization mentor newer professionals. This mentorship is invaluable for personal and professional development, providing guidance, career advice, and insights into handling complex cybersecurity challenges.
6. **Research and Innovation Projects**: Cybersecurity staff are encouraged to participate in research and innovation projects. These projects allow them to explore new technologies,

develop proprietary security solutions, and contribute to thought leadership in the cybersecurity community.

7. **Flexible Learning Paths**: Recognizing that learning is not one-size-fits-all, Organization A offers flexible learning paths including online courses, in-house training sessions, and self-directed learning options. This approach caters to different learning styles and allows professionals to develop at their own pace.
8. **Leadership Development Programs**: For those showing potential and interest in leadership roles, the company provides leadership development programs. These programs are aimed at grooming the next generation of cybersecurity leaders within the organization.

Organization A excels in providing their cybersecurity team with many opportunities for learning and growth, which significantly enhances their skill set and fosters high job satisfaction and a sense of professional accomplishment. This dedication to nurturing their team's development is a clear indication of their commitment to maintaining a leading-edge position in cybersecurity and fostering a culture that values continuous improvement and innovation. In an industry often plagued by high turnover rates in cybersecurity roles, Organization A stands out by aligning its cybersecurity objectives with the company's broader goals. This strategic integration not only boosts the effectiveness of their cybersecurity measures but also resonates with the career goals of their professionals. It creates a symbiotic relationship where the growth and advancement of individual team members contribute directly to the progress of the organization, and vice versa.

Organization B has established a highly effective and innovative approach to managing cybersecurity. Central to their success is a culture deeply rooted in teamwork and the sharing of knowledge. This approach aligns with the principles described in "You're a Leader, Charlie Brown" by Tracy, emphasizing the importance of collective leadership and the value of each team member's contributions. In this environment, every individual, regardless of their role or experience, is given the opportunity to lead and contribute meaningfully to the team's objectives. Organization B's recognition and reward system further reinforces this culture, resonating with the concepts in Ken Blanchard's "Servant Leadership in Action." The system at

Organization B is not just about acknowledging achievements; it also emphasizes the significance of teamwork, cooperation, and the extra effort team members make for the collective success of the cybersecurity initiatives. This approach to recognition serves as a powerful tool for motivation and encourages a mindset focused on collective success and continuous improvement. In terms of problem-solving, Organization B employs a variety of methodologies, ensuring a comprehensive approach to challenges, much like the strategies outlined in "The Leadership Secrets of Santa Claus" by Harvey. This method involves soliciting a wide range of perspectives and solutions, fostering creativity, and ensuring robust and effective cybersecurity measures. Furthermore, the execution of these strategies and ideas is managed with a disciplined approach, akin to the strategies in "The Four Disciplines of Execution" by Covey. Organization B places a strong emphasis on clearly defining goals, monitoring progress, and maintaining accountability. This disciplined execution ensures that innovative ideas and collaborative efforts are effectively implemented, leading to tangible and impactful results. Organization B's approach to cybersecurity management effectively combines innovative teamwork strategies, a comprehensive system of recognition, diverse problem-solving methodologies, and disciplined execution. This blend not only enhances their cybersecurity capabilities but also fosters a culture where teamwork, knowledge sharing, and continual improvement are integral to their operations.

Detailed Insights into Recognition and Reward System:

1. **Non-Monetary Recognition**: Organization B understands the impact of non-monetary recognition. Employees are often acknowledged in front of their peers during company-wide meetings, which boosts morale and fosters a sense of accomplishment. This public acknowledgment is not just limited to major achievements but also extends to consistent performance and small wins. Additionally, through internal newsletters, the company regularly features stories of individual and team successes in cybersecurity, providing an added layer of recognition and inspiring others. Note – some team members absolutely hate public recognition, make sure you know the preferences of the team members you are recognizing.
2. **Tangible Rewards**: Beyond verbal and written praise, tangible rewards play a significant role in their recognition strategy.

These rewards are carefully tailored to the achievements of the cybersecurity professionals. For instance, completing a crucial project might warrant a significant bonus, while resolving a more minor issue might be acknowledged with gift cards or an extra day off. This approach ensures that the rewards are meaningful and directly correlated to the level of contribution.

3. **Peer Recognition Programs**: The peer recognition program at Organization B is a testament to their collaborative culture. Colleagues regularly nominate each other for various recognitions, celebrating each other's contributions and successes. This peer-to-peer system strengthens team bonds and ensures that good work does not go unnoticed.
4. **Award for Continuous Learning**: Organization B places a high value on continuous learning and development. They have set up specific awards for team members who go beyond in their pursuit of knowledge. This could be acquiring new certifications, excelling in training programs, or even leading in-house knowledge-sharing sessions. These awards serve as motivation for the team to continually update their skills and stay ahead in the dynamic field of cybersecurity.

Expanding on Organization B's Problem-Solving Methodologies:

1. **Kepner-Tregoe Method**: The Kepner-Tregoe method, utilized by Organization B, is a systematic process that breaks down problems into manageable parts. This method is particularly beneficial in cybersecurity, where issues can be complex and multifaceted. By dissecting a problem and analyzing its root causes, the team can develop more effective and sustainable solutions.
2. **Winnie the Pooh on Problem Solving**: This unique approach, inspired by the beloved children's story, adds a creative twist to problem-solving. Team members adopt the characteristics of different characters from Winnie the Pooh to approach problems from various angles. For instance, adopting Rabbit's practicality or Tigger's enthusiasm can lead to diverse and innovative solutions. This method not only makes problem-solving sessions more engaging but also encourages thinking creatively.

3. **Regular "Hackathons"**: The internal hackathons organized by Organization B are a blend of competition and collaboration. These events simulate real-world cybersecurity scenarios, challenging the team to develop innovative solutions under pressure. This not only sharpens their technical skills but also promotes teamwork and quick thinking.
4. **Cross-functional Brainstorming Sessions**: By bringing together team members from different departments for brainstorming, Organization B ensures that cybersecurity solutions are well-rounded and consider various aspects of the business. This cross-functional approach leads to more comprehensive and effective cybersecurity strategies.

Organization B's innovative approach in blending recognition, rewards, and diverse problem-solving strategies plays a pivotal role in fostering a positive and dynamic work environment. This environment is instrumental in equipping their cybersecurity team with the tools and mindset essential for effectively tackling the complex challenges that come their way. The organization's focus on acknowledging and rewarding both individual achievements and collaborative efforts creates a culture of appreciation and motivation. This culture not only enhances job satisfaction but also drives team members to continually strive for excellence in their field. Their problem-solving methodologies, characterized by a blend of creativity and strategic thinking, ensure that the cybersecurity team is well-prepared to confront and adapt to the evolving nature of cybersecurity threats. By encouraging a proactive and collaborative approach to problem-solving, Organization B ensures that its solutions are robust, sustainable, and forward-thinking. The implementation of a disciplined and goal-oriented execution strategy ensures that innovative ideas and collaborative efforts are effectively translated into tangible outcomes. This focus on execution and accountability guarantees that the organization's strategic approach to cybersecurity yields impactful and measurable results. Organization B's comprehensive strategy in recognizing talent, encouraging innovative problem-solving, and fostering a culture of disciplined execution significantly contributes to their resilience and success in the competitive field of cybersecurity. This approach not only positions them as a leader in cybersecurity management but also as a model for other organizations striving to achieve excellence in this critical domain.

Organization C has crafted a cybersecurity culture that is exceptionally adaptive and resilient, setting a benchmark in how to retain and motivate top-tier cybersecurity talent. In a landscape where cyber threats evolve rapidly, their culture of adaptability and continuous improvement is not just beneficial but essential. This adaptability is fostered through a dynamic work environment that champions innovation and embraces change, making Organization C a standout in the field. Their approach to handling failure is particularly noteworthy. In many organizations, failure can be seen as a setback, but at Organization C, it is viewed as an invaluable learning opportunity. This perspective is crucial in an area as fast paced and ever-changing as cybersecurity. By reframing failures as steppingstones toward building stronger defenses, they have created an environment where cybersecurity professionals are not hindered by the fear of making mistakes. Instead, they are emboldened to innovate, experiment, and develop groundbreaking solutions to counter emerging threats. This approach aligns with the principles discussed in "The Leadership Secrets of Santa Claus" by Harvey, where embracing change and learning from experiences is key to success. Organization C has adopted a comprehensive and nuanced approach to understanding and addressing failures, a method that significantly contributes to their robust cybersecurity culture. Their methodology is not just about recognizing failures but about deeply understanding their nature and using them as a springboard for learning and improvement. Organization C categorizes failures into preventable, unavoidable, and intelligent. This categorization is vital as it helps the team understand that not all failures are equal, and each type provides distinct learning opportunities. Preventable failures, for instance, usually result from deviations from established protocols or standards. These are often the easiest to learn from, as they clearly highlight where processes can be improved. On the other hand, intelligent failures are viewed as valuable, especially in a field like cybersecurity where venturing into fresh territory is often necessary. These failures are seen as part of the learning process, essential for innovation and pushing the boundaries of current knowledge. At the heart of Organization C's approach is the development of an environment where team members feel secure and comfortable in admitting and discussing failures. Moving away from a blame-centric approach, they have cultivated a culture where failures are openly reported and constructively analyzed. This shift is fundamental in ensuring that failures are not hidden but are used as opportunities for collective learning and growth. They use a robust set of strategies for handling failure.

1. **Context-Specific Learning**: Organization C understands that each failure requires a tailored approach for analysis and learning. They encourage a deep and consistent analysis of failures to extract valuable lessons, ensuring that these insights are applied to prevent similar issues in the future.
2. **Fostering a Growth Mindset**: The organization promotes the perspective that failures are opportunities for learning. This mindset helps redefine setbacks as steppingstones toward success and encourages the sharing of lessons without fear of judgment.
3. **Encouraging Reflective Practices**: They facilitate personal reflection on contributions to failures, promoting ownership and responsibility. Reflective practices are key in identifying areas for personal and team growth, helping each member to understand their role in both the problem and the solution.
4. **Lead by Example in Learning from Failure**: Leadership at Organization C plays a critical role in building this learning culture. Leaders model the behavior they wish to see, emphasizing the importance of learning from mistakes and demonstrating resilience.
5. **Proactive Experimentation and Continuous Improvement**: The organization creates strategies that allow for safe risk-taking and experimentation. Failures are used to refine processes, systems, and strategies, always with an eye toward continuous improvement.
6. **Celebrate Efforts and Resilience**: Organization C recognizes and rewards not just successes but also the efforts and courage involved in trying new things. This approach helps in developing a team that is resilient, adaptable, and unafraid of facing new challenges.

Organization Cs detailed and thoughtful approach to handling failures – understanding their nature, creating a safe culture for discussion, implementing learning strategies, and fostering leadership and continuous improvement – is what sets them apart as a best-in-class example in cybersecurity. Their methods ensure that their team is not only equipped to handle current challenges but is also continuously evolving and improving, ready to meet the future demands of the cybersecurity landscape. Leadership at Organization C plays a critical role in this culture. They ensure that when failures occur, the focus is on analysis and learning, rather than blame. This aligns with the servant leadership principles from Ken Blanchard's "Servant Leadership in Action," fostering a supportive environment that values growth and learning from mistakes. By analyzing failures constructively, the organization not only improves its cybersecurity strategies but also builds a team that is more knowledgeable, resilient, and equipped to handle future challenges. Organization C's culture of adaptability, innovation, and learning from failure is why Organization C excels in retaining and motivating their cybersecurity talent. They recognize that in the ever-evolving world of cyber threats, a static approach is inadequate. Instead, they have created an environment that encourages continuous enhancement and growth. This not only leads to more robust cybersecurity defenses but also to a workforce that is engaged, motivated, and loyal. The result is a reduced turnover rate and a team that remains committed to protecting the organization against the growing range of cyber threats. The accomplishments of Organization C in establishing a positive and supportive cybersecurity culture stand as a prime example of the critical importance of such an investment. This culture is not solely about safeguarding the organization from the myriads of cyber threats that exist in today's digital world. It goes beyond this defensive stance to play a pivotal role in fostering a team that is not only continually motivated but also thoroughly prepared to navigate the complexities inherent in the cybersecurity field. Organization C has masterfully struck a balance between fostering innovation, encouraging adaptability, and embracing the valuable lessons that come from facing and overcoming challenges. This balanced approach is what elevates Organization C, distinguishing it as a model for best practices in cybersecurity talent retention and motivation. The success of Organization C serves as a powerful testament to the fact that a robust cybersecurity culture is about much more than just technical defenses. It is about creating an environment where cybersecurity professionals feel valued, are encouraged to grow, and are equipped to handle the challenges that come their way. This environment ensures that the professionals are not just competent in their technical roles but are also deeply invested in the overall mission and vision of the organization. It creates a sense of belonging and purpose, factors that are critical in retaining talent in an industry often characterized by high turnover rates.

A strong cybersecurity culture is essential for building resilient, high-performing, and motivated teams. It is not just about safeguarding assets but also about creating an environment where individuals feel empowered, valued, and inspired to contribute their best efforts. Leadership plays a pivotal role in fostering this culture by championing values of trust, transparency, and continuous learning. Empowering cybersecurity professionals involves more than technical training, it requires equipping them with opportunities for growth, recognition, and collaboration. Advanced training programs, mentorship, and flexible learning paths keep team members at the forefront of industry trends, while recognition programs celebrate their achievements and encourage innovation. Acknowledging and rewarding both individual and team successes builds morale and reinforces a sense of purpose and shared responsibility. Mistakes and failures are inevitable in a dynamic field like cybersecurity, but they should be seen as learning opportunities and steppingstones to greater strength and adaptability. Cultivating a culture where experimentation is encouraged, and setbacks are reframed as learning opportunities promotes resilience and drives innovation. This approach fosters a fearless mindset, empowering professionals to tackle evolving threats with creativity and confidence. Leadership is the foundation upon which this culture is built. Leaders who model the behaviors they wish to inspire, whether through collaboration, inclusivity, or a commitment to growth set the tone for their teams. By investing in the development of their people and fostering an environment that balances accountability with support, leaders ensure long-term team success and retention. A robust cybersecurity culture unites the organization's mission with the individual aspirations of its team members. By prioritizing trust, continuous improvement, and recognition, organizations can create teams that are resilient, engaged, and prepared to excel in the face of ever-evolving cyber threats.

Chapter 4 Notable Passages and key points

- *"In this environment, cybersecurity professionals are not confined to traditional roles of safeguarding digital assets. They are encouraged to contribute creatively to the company's growth, transforming them from mere defenders into innovators and strategic assets."*
- *Empowering cybersecurity teams with a culture of trust, continuous learning, and resilience enables them to innovate fearlessly, adapt to evolving threats, and remain motivated to achieve excellence in protecting organizational assets."*
  - Integrating growth and innovation into cybersecurity roles transforms defenders into strategic assets.
  - Recognition, collaboration, and shared responsibility create resilient and motivated teams.
  - A culture that embraces failures as learning opportunities fosters innovation and adaptability.

5

Practical Advice for Creating the Pillars of Cybersecurity Culture Trust, Respect, and Purpose

Trust is a two-way street, earned by both leaders and team members through genuine interactions and mutual respect. It's about aligning actions with words and creating a collaborative space where people can grow, contribute, and feel part of a larger mission.

– Kevin Lynn McLaughlin, PhD

Building a strong culture in the field of cybersecurity is more than just a strategic advantage; it is a necessity for talent retention, motivation, and job satisfaction. At its core, such a culture revolves around creating an environment that resonates with the values, ambitions, and professional needs of cybersecurity professionals. A culture that wins the hearts and minds of cybersecurity talent is one where each member feels genuinely valued and respected. This is not just about acknowledging their contributions but also about understanding their unique perspectives, wants and skills. Farber's concepts in "Radical LEAP" (Love, Energy, Audacity, and Proof) apply here. Treating each team member with love and respect creates a foundation of trust and mutual respect, crucial in a field as dynamic and challenging as cybersecurity. Incorporating the principle of 'being here now' is vital. Cybersecurity teams often work in high-pressure environments, dealing with evolving threats and complex problems. A culture that emphasizes being fully present and engaged not only improves focus and efficiency but also ensures that team members feel heard and understood. This approach fosters open communication and a

DOI: 10.1201/9781003462064-5

collaborative spirit, essential for innovative problem-solving. One of the first things that I do with new teams is ask that laptops not be brought into meetings. Close your eyes for a second and just think about the responses I get from most people to that request. While I know that this can bother a few of the team members that are taking notes on their system, the reality is that an open laptop, regardless of the best of intentions tends to lead to checking into email and checking out of the meeting. If a team member really does take notes electronically for their preferred filing system, buy them a notepad that synchronizes up to their electronic storage area. In the spirit of be here now, my mantra on meetings is clear and to the point, I make exceptions to this rule but not often:

- In almost every instance only one team member is needed in meetings (I am not referring to workshops and strategy sessions here- those are different) and they can provide updates to the other team members who need the information.
- Be present if you choose to attend a meeting. That means no laptop and no staring at your phone the whole time. If you cannot be present, then just do not go to the meeting.
- And the most important one – just because someone invites you to a meeting does not mean you have to attend. When in doubt pick up the phone and ask why your attendance is required so you can make an informed decision about attending.

Developing a robust cybersecurity culture involves more than just day-to-day tasks; it requires an overarching vision where every team member understands and aligns with the end goals. This concept, inspired by Stephen Covey's "Seven Habits," particularly focuses on setting clear, impactful goals, often termed as "Blue Chip" or "big rocks." In a cybersecurity context, these "big rocks" represent two to three significant objectives each team member should aim to achieve annually. These are not ordinary tasks but pivotal goals that contribute to advancing the team's mission. These items make a difference and move the dial for the organization. The essence of this approach is to ensure that all individual's efforts are not just about ticking off a list of tasks but about making a meaningful difference that aligns with the broader objectives of the cybersecurity department. Such a focus on significant, impactful goals takes a shared vision within the team. It is about ensuring that everyone is not just working but are collectively working toward the same end. This shared vision acts as a road map, helping to align individual efforts and aspirations with the mission of the team. It is about creating a sense of purpose and direction, which is particularly crucial in the dynamic and often reactive field of cybersecurity. Leaders in cybersecurity play a crucial role in this process. They are responsible for clearly articulating these “Blue Chips” and ensuring that each team member understands how their individual goals fit into the larger picture. This practice goes beyond mere task assignment; it involves inspiring the team, fostering a sense of ownership, and encouraging each team member to see how their contributions directly impact the team’s success and, by extension, the security posture of the entire organization. It also allows team members to say no to meetings and other activities that are not aligned with any of the 30-40 blue chips that span across the team. It is said that only 20% of what most people do in a day is important to a team’s overall success. Leveraging Blue Chips in the manner described increases that percentage and gives the team members much more overall satisfaction in their accomplishments. Embedding the principle of keeping ‘the end in mind’ into the foundation of your cybersecurity culture is about more than just setting goals. It is about cultivating a shared vision, focusing on impactful objectives, and ensuring that all team member’s efforts contribute meaningfully toward achieving the overarching mission of the cybersecurity team. This approach not only drives efficiency and effectiveness but also instills a sense of purpose, ownership, and cohesion within the team. Cybersecurity is not only about protecting data and assets; it is about safeguarding the integrity and reputation of the organization and ensuring the trust of customers and stakeholders. When team members understand and have goals that directly relate to the larger purpose and impact of their work, they are more likely to feel motivated and aligned with the organization’s objectives.

In “Winning Teams, Winning Cultures,” the concept of mood elevators is discussed to understand how leaders can effectively shape and influence the cultural dynamics of their teams. This concept is particularly pertinent in the high-stress, high-stakes world of cybersecurity. Mood elevators are tools or practices that help individuals manage and more importantly acknowledge their emotional states, in meetings and particularly in challenging situations. In cybersecurity, where the pressure to protect against threats and respond to incidents is constant, the mood of team members within the team can significantly impact performance, decision-making, and collaboration. Leaders in cybersecurity can use mood elevators to cultivate a positive and resilient team environment. This involves encouraging a mindset that focuses on solutions rather than dwelling on problems. A mood elevator is not only used to decide if you should postpone a meeting because you are feeling low in the mood elevator or have the meeting because you are at an elevated level on the mood elevator. In *The Mood Elevator: Take Charge of Your Feelings, Become a Better You*, Larry Senn introduces the Mood Elevator as a metaphorical framework that maps the spectrum of human emotions, ranging from higher levels like gratitude, curiosity, and creativity to lower states such as frustration, irritation, and despair. This emphasizes the importance of self-awareness and emotional regulation, offering practical strategies to navigate one's mood and positively influence others. In cybersecurity, where high-pressure situations and rapid decision-making are the norm, the Mood Elevator can serve as a valuable tool for shaping team dynamics and fostering resilience. The key idea behind the Mood Elevator is that emotional states are transient and can be managed through conscious effort. Leaders who understand this can model behaviors that align with the higher floors of the Mood Elevator; demonstrating optimism, resourcefulness, and patience; even when faced with challenges. By doing so, they set a tone that permeates throughout the team, creating an environment where individuals feel supported and motivated. In cybersecurity, where the stakes are high, this emotional leadership can mean the difference between a team that reacts with panic and one that responds with clarity and focus. Senn emphasizes the role of "pattern interrupts" as a mechanism for shifting from lower to higher emotional states. For cybersecurity leaders, this might involve pausing during a crisis to reframe the problem as an opportunity for learning or innovation. Instead of succumbing to frustration during a security breach, a leader using the Mood Elevator might ask the team to reflect on what went right and how future incidents can be better mitigated. This constructive focus not only elevates morale but also fosters a culture of continuous improvement. Another crucial element of the Mood Elevator is its impact on communication and collaboration. Leaders who are attuned to their own emotional states and those of their team members are better equipped to facilitate meaningful interactions. For instance, during high-stress moments, acknowledging and validating the team's emotions can defuse tension and build trust. Incorporating the principles of the Mood Elevator into leadership practices in cybersecurity also aligns closely with concepts from Stephen R. Covey's *The 7 Habits of Highly Effective People*, particularly the habit of being proactive. Just as Covey advocates for taking responsibility for one's reactions and mindset, the Mood Elevator encourages individuals to take charge of their emotional well-being. This approach not only enhances individual performance but also strengthens the overall culture, creating a team that thrives even under the pressure of an evolving threat landscape. Ultimately, the Mood Elevator is more than just a theoretical concept; it is a practical framework for cultivating emotional intelligence and resilience. For cybersecurity leaders, it offers a way to navigate the emotional complexities of their role while fostering an environment where trust, collaboration, and innovation can flourish. By elevating their own mood and that of their team, leaders ensure that challenges are met with clarity, unity, and a shared commitment to excellence.

In addition to making use of the mood elevator levels leaders must create *effective communication channels*, regular check-ins, and a supportive atmosphere where team members can express concerns or stress without fear of judgment. This openness not only helps in early identification and mitigation of potential issues but also strengthens the team's cohesion and trust. Incorporating effective and positive communication into the team culture requires leading by example. Leaders who demonstrate positivity, resilience, and a purposeful approach in their own behavior set the tone for the rest of the team. These leaders become role models for how to manage stress and challenges effectively. Which in turn helps the team members do the same, less stress and frustration can often lead to less turn-over. **A personal story** – one of the first things I do when I inherit or get the honor of leading a new team is to contact each team member to say hello and learn a little bit about him or her. This call is a short one 10–15 minutes depending on the team size and is used to start laying the foundation of an open and trusting relationship. Once, when I called a Senior Analyst, we were only into the virtual meeting for a minute, and I noticed that he was crying. I stopped and asked what was wrong and I will never forget what he told me. He said, "I have been working her for 20 years and I have never had any Senior leader (Director or Above) call and just ask how I was doing or how my family was doing." They only call when something is wrong. Take a moment and think about that. I apologized to him on behalf of his previous leaders. *If you do not take the time to know your people, they have no reason to work for you or to stay working for you*, with currently 3.5 million openings for Cybersecurity professionals they have many other options.

Trust is the cornerstone of effective leadership and team dynamics, particularly in the demanding field of cybersecurity. Covey's "Trust Works" and the insights from "Crucial Conversations" by Patterson, Grenny, McMillan, and Switzler provide valuable frameworks for understanding and building trust. Covey in "Trust Works" emphasizes the importance of being genuine in building trust. He suggests that trust is not just a soft, social virtue but rather a hard, economic driver for organizations. Trust is a measurable accelerator to performance, affecting speed and cost in every dimension of business. When leaders are genuine, they create an environment of transparency and openness, which fosters trust among team members. For instance, a cybersecurity leader who openly shares information, admits mistakes, and treats others fairly, even under pressure, will earn the trust of their team.

- **Openly Sharing Information**: Regularly updating the team about the latest threats, changes in security protocols, or new tools and technologies. Imagine a team meeting where the leader discusses a recently attempted security breach, not just to highlight the threat but also to explain how it was identified and neutralized. This transparency helps the team understand the current landscape and feel more involved in the overall strategy.
- **Admitting Mistakes**: This trait is crucial, especially in a field where errors can have significant consequences. A leader might call a meeting to review a security incident that was mishandled, openly acknowledging their own oversight or misjudgment in the situation. For example, a patch was

delayed under their decision, leading to an exploited vulnerability. By admitting this mistake, the leader not only demonstrates accountability but also turns the situation into a learning opportunity for the entire team.

- **Treating Others Fairly, Even Under Pressure**: Cybersecurity environments can be high-pressure, especially during a security incident.

  (I once received a screen shot from someone working a ransomware recovery, they were 3 days in of sitting and working recovery solutions. The screenshot showed their sitting heartrate at 135, that's right, the stress was so high that their sitting heartrate was as high as if they had gone out for a run.)

  In such situations, a leader must maintain composure and make decisions based on objective criteria, rather than playing favorites or assigning blame. For instance, if a team member fails to detect a phishing attempt leading to a breach, the leader avoids singling them out for blame. Instead, they would focus on understanding the lapse and how the team can collectively prevent such occurrences in the future.

"Crucial Conversations" offers further insights, particularly in how effective communication is integral to trust-building. It highlights the importance of dialogue, especially in high-stakes situations. Leaders who master the art of crucial conversations create a psychologically safe environment where all team members can contribute their opinions and feel heard. This is particularly important in cybersecurity, where the stakes are high, and decisions often must be made quickly. By encouraging open dialogue, leaders demonstrate their respect for their team's expertise and perspectives, thereby building trust. These conversations are not about being nice but about being honest and straightforward, even when discussing difficult topics. This kind of openness in communication not only resolves potential misunderstandings but also strengthens relationships, thereby building a solid foundation of trust. Having conversations that are honest and straightforward, even about difficult topics, is crucial for building trust and strong relationships within a team. These conversations go beyond just being nice; they require a level of candor and openness that can sometimes be challenging but beneficial.

- Consider a situation where a team member repeatedly fails to follow established security protocols. A straightforward conversation in this case would not just be a polite reminder but a clear discussion about the potential risks their actions pose to the organization. The leader would explain the consequences of such lapses, not just in terms of security breaches but also in terms of the team's trust and the company's reputation. This conversation, while tough, underscores the seriousness of the issue and the need for adherence to protocols.
- Another scenario might involve addressing budget cuts or resource limitations that affect the cybersecurity team. Instead of sugarcoating the issue, a leader should honestly communicate the challenges and the impact it might have on the team's operations. They might discuss the need to prioritize certain projects over others or explore alternative solutions like open-source tools or cross-training team members to manage multiple roles. This level of transparency helps the team understand the bigger picture and prepares them to adapt to changes.
- In cases of security incidents, an honest and direct conversation is even more critical. If an incident occurs due to a team member's oversight, the discussion should focus on what went wrong, the learnings from the incident, and the steps to prevent such occurrences in the future. Instead of assigning blame, the emphasis should be on collective responsibility and improvement.

Hopefully, these examples illustrate how straightforward communication can help resolve misunderstandings and issues more effectively than avoiding or glossing over them. By being honest and direct, leaders not only address problems head-on but also demonstrate respect for their team's ability to handle and contribute to tough conversations. This approach fosters a culture of openness, encourages the sharing of ideas and concerns, and builds a solid foundation of trust within the team. Fostering an environment where open, spirited, and direct conversations can thrive is an essential part of building a resilient and innovative cybersecurity team. Each year, I intentionally create opportunities for team members to engage in these types of discussions to strengthen their ability to communicate openly and constructively, a skill as vital as any technical proficiency in the cybersecurity profession. One particularly memorable example is an event we hold annually: our invite-only "Fight Night." During this event, we tackle three forward-thinking cybersecurity topics in an unstructured, lively debate format. The lack of formal rules encourages creativity, bluntness, and the type of spirited engagement that often leads to breakthrough ideas. While it can take some time for team members to acclimate to the freewheeling nature of Fight Night, the results speak for themselves. These discussions challenge assumptions, spark new perspectives, and deepen the team's ability to handle complex, high-pressure situations collaboratively. Of course, Fight Night is only one piece of the puzzle. Throughout the year, we also conduct numerous structured and organized conversations to ensure that all voices are heard, and that collaboration remains productive. However, Fight Night holds a special place in our culture because it serves as an accelerator for building the muscle to engage in direct and meaningful dialogue. I will likely hear some playful grief from my team for even mentioning it; after all, the first rule of Fight Night is that we don't talk about Fight Night. But its impact on our team's ability to innovate, challenge one another respectfully, and approach problems with fresh perspectives cannot be overstated.

A cybersecurity leader's success with retention must encompass two key practices: aligning actions with their words and recognizing the demanding work of their team.

- Walk the Talk
- Focused, Individualized Recognition

Let us imagine a leader who talks about the importance of following cybersecurity protocols. It is one thing to say it, but it is another to do it. For instance, if they stress the importance of updating software regularly, they should be the first to update their own systems. This kind of behavior sets a strong example for the team. It is not just about giving orders; it is about being part of the team and showing that you are all in this together. When the team sees their leader walking the talk, it builds trust and shows that the leader is committed and dependable. When it comes to recognizing the team's efforts it is important to be genuine and know how your employees prefer to be recognized. Some employees love public recognition while others hate public recognition, do not be the leader who puts the latter on stage to recognize them. *Keep in mind that recognition is not about you, it is about the team member and should be presented in a form and format that they will appreciate.* In cybersecurity, a lot of the work goes unnoticed, especially when it involves preventing problems. But a good leader sees these efforts and makes sure they are acknowledged. Say a team member spots and stops a phishing attack, or someone leads the implementation of a new security tool that really boosts the company's defenses. These achievements are worth celebrating. Mentioning these successes in the manner that resonates with the team member not only boosts morale but also shows the team that their hard work is valued and crucial. This kind of acknowledgment encourages everyone to keep up the excellent work and fosters a sense of pride in their roles. A cybersecurity leader who practices what they preach and recognizes their team's contributions is more likely to build a strong, trusting team. This approach is essential in cybersecurity, where teamwork and dedication play vital roles in protecting the company's digital assets. Trust is built on the pillars of genuineness, effective communication, consistency, and recognition. Leaders in cybersecurity, or any field for that matter, who embrace these principles are more likely to create a high-trust, high-performing team.

Professional growth and continuous learning are also central to building your culture. Cybersecurity is a rapidly evolving field, and a culture that prioritizes learning and development will not only keep the team updated with the latest trends and technologies but also signal to the professionals that their growth is valued. This could be through regular training, workshops, or even encouraging participation in industry conferences and forums. A culture that wins in cybersecurity is one that recognizes and rewards innovation and initiative even while successfully maintaining a strongly controlled environment. Cybersecurity professionals thrive in environments where they can experiment, take calculated risks, and bring innovative ideas to the table. Acknowledging and rewarding these efforts reinforces a culture of innovation and continuous improvement. A strong culture in cybersecurity is one that is built on respect, engagement, purpose, positivity, learning, and innovation. It is an environment where team members feel valued, their contributions are recognized, and they are empowered to grow and excel in their roles. Such a culture not only attracts top talent but also nurtures and retains them, creating a cycle of success and satisfaction.

1. **Cultivating a Collaborative and Inclusive Environment**:
   - **Weekly Team Breakfasts or Lunches**: Regular team breakfasts can serve as an informal setting for employees to connect and discuss non-work-related topics, fostering camaraderie. Encourage open invitations for team members to dine with the cybersecurity leadership team. This breaks down hierarchical barriers and promotes open communication. Keep in mind that this breakfast is not about you, many of your team members have kids to get off to school, workouts to finish, and other morning events. Start your open, eat breakfast with the Leadership Team (LT) at 9AM and have it open to anyone on the team who is onsite and wants to attend. Remember, your team members are busy, do not make this recurring event mandatory or make it too early in the morning. Worst case is you have a nice breakfast by yourself that you can use for planning and thinking. Yes, these events can be virtual if you have a lot of remote team members.
2. **Understanding and Supporting Individual Goals**:
   - **Personalized Career Path Discussions**: Knowing each team member's future goals and providing support in achieving them is crucial. Regular one-on-one discussions to discuss career aspirations and necessary skills development can boost morale and loyalty. Once you know what a team member's future goals are then you need to help develop opportunities for them that tie into and help them reach those goals. Training opportunities, conferences, getting in front of the correct leaders, individual coaching, and think tank sessions are some examples.
3. **Fostering a Learning Mindset**:
   - **Celebrating Failures as Learning Opportunities**: Celebrating failures as learning opportunities is a critical aspect of fostering a culture of growth and resilience in

cybersecurity. Initial failures, especially when navigating uncharted territories or tackling complex challenges, are natural parts of the learning curve. Leaders who emphasize the value of these experiences demonstrate that setbacks are not endpoints but steppingstones toward innovation and improvement. Drawing from *Mindset* by Carol Dweck, adopting a growth mindset encourages team members to view failures as opportunities to develop new skills and refine strategies. This approach fosters creativity and problem-solving, as individuals are less afraid to take calculated risks. In cybersecurity, where evolving threats demand innovation, this mindset is crucial for staying ahead of adversaries. At the same time, accountability must balance this openness to learning. As highlighted in *The Discipline of Teams* by Jon Katzenbach and Douglas Smith, a strong team culture requires that repetitive mistakes be addressed constructively. By creating an environment where feedback is specific and solutions-focused, leaders reinforce the importance of learning from errors while ensuring continuous improvement. Celebrating failures also involves recognizing the courage it takes to try new approaches, even if they don't succeed. Leaders can model this by sharing their own missteps and the lessons they've gained, building trust and setting an example. However, addressing recurring issues constructively ensures that the team maintains high standards of accountability and professionalism. By striking this balance, organizations create a resilient culture that values both learning and excellence.

4. **Authentic Leadership and Role Modeling**:
   - **'Walk the Talk'**: Leadership must exemplify the behaviors they expect from their team. Actions often speak louder than words in establishing a culture of trust and respect.
   - **Adopting Strong Cultural Baselines**: Implementing frameworks like those taught by Senn Delaney provides a structured approach to shaping organizational culture, emphasizing the alignment of behaviors with organizational values. This intentional focus fosters trust, collaboration, and accountability, key elements in high-stakes fields like cybersecurity. Insights from "*The 21 Irrefutable Laws*

of Leadership" by John Maxwell reinforce the idea that effective leadership sets the ceiling for organizational success. Leaders who intentionally adopt cultural frameworks can elevate team potential, creating environments where individuals thrive, and collective goals are met. Similarly, *Servant Leadership in Action* by Ken Blanchard highlights the power of service-oriented leadership, where leaders prioritize clarity, resources, and support to cultivate empowerment and trust. The concept of focusing outward, as explored in *Leadership and Self-Deception* by the Arbinger Institute, complements structured cultural approaches. Leaders who prioritize the needs of their teams over personal agendas foster collaboration and mutual respect which is essential for high-performing cultures. By integrating these insights with structured cultural frameworks, organizations ensure their culture aligns with strategic goals, fostering a cohesive, mission-driven environment where teams can excel.

5. **Respect and Empathy in Interactions**:
   - **Treating People as You Would Like to Be Treated**: Treating people as you would like to be treated is a cornerstone of fostering respect and empathy within a team. This principle is especially vital in cybersecurity, where high-pressure situations demand strong collaboration and trust. Respect means valuing the unique contributions and perspectives of every team member, while empathy ensures understanding and support, particularly during challenging times. In *Dare to Lead* by Brené Brown, the importance of fostering vulnerability-based trust highlights how respect and empathy create a safe space for honest communication. Similarly, *Servant Leadership* by Robert Greenleaf emphasizes that treating individuals with dignity and care builds stronger, more loyal teams. Leaders who embody these principles enhance collaboration and morale, enabling teams to respond more effectively to cybersecurity challenges. Applying respect and empathy extends to creating supportive policies, like flexible work arrangements and recognition programs, which demonstrate an organization's commitment to its people. These

actions not only promote individual well-being but also strengthen the cohesion and resilience of the entire team, paving the way for long-term success.

6. **Focus on Results, Not Just Presence**:
   In a high-performing cybersecurity culture, success is measured by outcomes and deliverables rather than time spent in the office. This results-driven approach emphasizes productivity and impact, ensuring that the focus remains on meaningful contributions rather than rigid schedules. Setting clear objectives and defining measurable goals (such as individual Blue Chips) allows team members to prioritize effectively, aligning their efforts with organizational priorities. This approach also promotes a healthier work-life balance, reducing burnout while fostering trust and accountability. When professionals feel their work is evaluated on results rather than hours logged, they are more likely to take ownership, innovate, and perform at their best. Leaders reinforce this culture by recognizing achievements based on outcomes, modeling a commitment to quality and efficiency. By valuing results over presence, organizations empower their teams to excel, ensuring both professional satisfaction and the ability to meet evolving cybersecurity challenges effectively.
7. **Active Participation in Meetings**:
   Creating a culture of active engagement is crucial for the success of a cybersecurity team. Every team member must understand the value of their voice and the importance of contributing to discussions. Passive attendance in meetings is not enough; it is through active participation that the most effective problem-solving and decision-making occurs. We hire exceptional individuals because we trust their intelligence, insights, and abilities to improve the cybersecurity organization. When a team member remains silent during discussions, they are not only withholding their unique perspective but also failing to uphold the collaborative ethos that drives the team's success. This behavior, while often unintentional, undermines the cultural expectations of contribution and engagement that are essential for a high-performing team. At the same time, it's important for team members to understand that sharing

their ideas does not always guarantee implementation. The value lies in the act of contributing, of adding to the collective knowledge and pushing the boundaries of the discussion. A healthy culture ensures that every idea is considered and respected, even if not every idea is adopted. By reinforcing this dynamic, team members feel both valued and encouraged to contribute, knowing their voices are integral to the team's success, regardless of the immediate outcomes.

8. **Clarity in Objectives and Expectations: (Blue Chips)**: While the concept of "blue chips" has been explored earlier, it is worth revisiting their importance as a foundational element for aligning individual efforts with the broader mission and vision of a cybersecurity team. Clearly articulating objectives and expectations ensures that every team member understands their role within the larger framework of the organization's goals. The habit of "beginning with the end in mind" highlights the value of defining significant priorities. In the context of cybersecurity, blue chips represent these high-impact priorities, key deliverables that anchor the team's focus amidst the dynamic and fast-paced challenges of the field. By outlining these objectives, leaders provide clarity and purpose, ensuring efforts are directed toward meaningful outcomes rather than scattered tasks. Equally critical, as discussed in Katzenbach and Smith's *The Discipline of Teams*, is ensuring that objectives resonate with individual team members. Leaders should tie each blue chip to personal growth opportunities, creating a sense of ownership and intrinsic motivation. When individuals see how their contributions impact the organization's success, it fosters alignment, accountability, and a shared commitment to excellence. Leaders must revisit and refine these objectives as conditions evolve, ensuring they remain relevant and actionable. It is the continuous reinforcement and connection to the broader vision that keeps blue chips integral to both individual and collective success. By focusing on clearly articulated blue chips, organizations establish a guiding compass for their cybersecurity teams, one that not only enhances strategic alignment but also cultivates a mo-

tivated and purpose-driven workforce prepared to meet the complexities of an ever-changing threat landscape.

9. **Measuring Success and Effectiveness**:
   Measuring the effectiveness of culture-building efforts is essential to ensure organizational initiatives align with team needs and goals. Key metrics such as employee turnover rates, job satisfaction scores, and regular survey feedback offer valuable insights into the health of a cybersecurity team's culture. Employee turnover rates highlight retention success, with high turnover often signaling engagement or morale issues. Job satisfaction scores reflect how team members perceive their work environment and leadership, while regular surveys provide actionable insights into team experiences. As emphasized in *Cybersecurity Metrics* by Andrew Jaquith, using clear, quantifiable metrics is crucial for tracking progress and driving informed decision-making. By consistently monitoring these metrics, leaders can evaluate the impact of their culture-building efforts and make data-driven adjustments that foster a resilient, engaged team environment.

The creation of a robust culture in cybersecurity is not a one-off task but an ongoing process. It requires commitment, consistency, and a genuine interest in the well-being and professional growth of the team members. By implementing these strategies, organizations can build a strong, resilient, and motivated cybersecurity team, capable of facing the dynamic challenges of the cybersecurity landscape. The success of any strategy or methodology ultimately hinges on how we lead and interact with our teams. Leadership in cybersecurity demands trust, trust in the professionalism, judgment, and discretion of team members. When a team member chooses not to attend a meeting, the default response should be one of confidence in their decision. Criticizing or doubting their choice only undermines the autonomy and respect necessary for fostering a healthy, high-functioning culture. This principle extends to email communication, where overusing CC, and especially BCC, stems from a culture of fear rather than trust. BCC'ing, except in rare cases like masking recipient lists, undermines transparency and can erode team cohesion and negatively impact team culture. Leaders should foster an environment that values direct, pertinent updates over defensive overcommunication. By modeling trust and clarity, they reduce unnecessary noise and create a culture focused on meaningful collaboration rather than fear of missteps. Leaders who expect to be looped in on every detail risk creating a toxic environment where team members operate defensively rather than productively. Instead of demanding omniscience through email chains, leaders should prioritize direct and respectful communication. If something needs clarification or further insight, simply ask. Respecting professional discretion and fostering direct communication are hallmarks of an effective and supportive team culture. These practices not only build trust but also empower team members to focus on meaningful contributions rather than operating in fear of being second-guessed or micromanaged. *As leaders, we must model this approach, creating a culture where accountability thrives alongside autonomy.*

Equally important is understanding and empathy when team members balance work with personal commitments. For instance, if a team member is attending a significant family event like a child's holiday concert, it is essential to respect their commitment to family, even if it means they cannot immediately respond to work communications. As a leader, your focus needs to be more on whether they deliver, and whether they do so in a way that meets our cultural expectations. Your focus should not be on whether they sat at their desk from 8-5 being busy versus being productive. In line with this, it is important to recognize that trust is a two-way street, earned by both the leader and the team member. If a team member consistently makes poor decisions or shows a lack of sound judgment, this issue needs to be addressed promptly and respectfully. It is not about punishment, but about providing the necessary coaching and mentoring to guide them back on track. This process is vital in maintaining the integrity and efficiency of the team. For example, if a team member repeatedly skips meetings that they should be attending, a leader should provide specific, constructive feedback and additional training. The goal is to help them understand the impact of their actions and improve their performance. Addressing these issues swiftly and respectfully ensures that the cybersecurity team's high standards are maintained, while also reinforcing that everyone is supported in their professional growth and development. A personal experience highlights the significance of empathy and trust in leadership. I once faced the heart-wrenching situation of losing a parent. Though I was assured by my leader that taking time off to sit at my mother's bedside during her last days was acceptable, this same leader, who I had trusted, later used my 4-day absence to negatively impact my annual performance evaluation. This incident underscores a fundamental truth: the principles and strategies we discuss are most effective in an environment of mutual respect and trust. I resigned the next day as that was not the type of person I could work with. The way we treat our team members in their times of need, in their moments of balancing personal and professional responsibilities, profoundly impacts not only their performance but the overall morale and effectiveness of the team.

Building a cohesive and resilient culture in cybersecurity requires far more than technical expertise or operational strategies. It demands an unwavering commitment to trust, respect, and mutual understanding as foundational principles. Throughout this chapter, the focus has been on how leaders shape the environment where cybersecurity teams can thrive. Leadership in this space is not just about solving technical problems or making strategic decisions; it is about inspiring and supporting people to reach their fullest potential. Trust stands as a cornerstone of effective leadership. It is not granted automatically but earned through consistent and authentic actions. Leaders must align their behavior with the standards they set, demonstrating reliability, fairness, and integrity. When leaders embody the values they expect from their teams, they foster a culture of accountability and mutual respect. This trust, once established, allows team members to feel secure in their roles and confident in their leader's guidance. Recognizing and appreciating the contributions of team members is another essential element of strong team culture. Cybersecurity professionals often work in high-pressure environments where their efforts to prevent threats or mitigate risks can go unseen. Taking the time to acknowledge these contributions boosts morale, reinforces purpose, and creates a sense of belonging. Importantly, recognition should be tailored to individual preferences, some team members value public acknowledgment, while others may appreciate more private or personalized gestures. Understanding these preferences demonstrates a leader's empathy and commitment to the team's well-being. Trust must also flow in both directions. Leaders must extend trust to their team members, empowering them to make decisions and take ownership of their responsibilities. This trust is especially important when mistakes occur. Effective leaders address errors constructively, viewing them as opportunities for learning and growth rather than reasons for blame. Constructive feedback and mentoring ensure that setbacks are transformed into teachable moments, fostering a culture of continuous improvement. By handling mistakes with understanding and support, leaders build confidence and resilience within the team.

Open and transparent communication emerged as another critical theme. Leaders set the tone for collaboration by encouraging dialogue, listening actively, and being clear about expectations. This openness invites team members to share their ideas, voice concerns, and engage fully with the mission, enriching the team's overall effectiveness. Communication, when practiced effectively, becomes a tool for building trust, aligning efforts, and ensuring that every voice is heard. *Ultimately, the strength of any cybersecurity team lies in its people.* While technology and processes play important roles, it is the expertise, dedication, and collaboration of the team that form the foundation of an effective security program. Leaders who invest in building a culture rooted in trust, respect, and empowerment enable their teams to perform at their best even in the face of complex and evolving challenges. Reflecting on these principles, it becomes clear that *the true measure of leadership in cybersecurity is not just in technical expertise but in the ability to inspire, engage, and uplift a team.* A culture that prioritizes these values does more than enhancing performance; it creates a lasting foundation for long-term success and satisfaction, both for the team and the organization they protect.

Chapter 5 Notable Passages and key points

- *"As a leader in cybersecurity, your actions and behaviors must mirror the principles and standards you set for your team. It's your consistent alignment between what you say and what you do that builds trust and establishes your credibility as a leader."*
- *"Recognizing and valuing the contributions of each team member is not just a nice gesture; it's a fundamental aspect of building a cohesive and motivated team. Tailoring this recognition to individual preferences and contributions significantly boosts morale and fosters a sense of belonging within the cybersecurity team."*

- Trust is built through genuine leadership, consistent actions, and open communication.
- A culture of purpose aligns individual contributions with organizational goals, fostering motivation and engagement.
- Recognition tailored to individual preferences strengthens team morale and a sense of belonging.

6

Servant Leadership, Positive Energy, and Trust in Cybersecurity

In cybersecurity, we lead not just by managing, but by inspiring and empowering our team to excel. Our strength lies in nurturing their growth and facing challenges together.

– Kevin Lynn McLaughlin, PhD

The role of a cybersecurity leader is not just to manage and direct their team, but to inspire, motivate, and support their professionals in their development and growth. As such, it is essential for cybersecurity leaders to adopt a servant leadership approach, lead with positive energy, and build trust across their organization. Servant leadership is a leadership philosophy in which the leader places the needs and growth of their team members above their own. By doing so, they create a supportive and empowering work environment that encourages their professionals to succeed and thrive. This leadership style is particularly important in the field of cybersecurity, where professionals are constantly facing new and complex challenges. Drawing from "The Wisdom of Bullfrog Leadership," servant leadership in cybersecurity is about doing the right things for the right reasons, which resonates with honor as the foundation of great leadership. The approach is defined as accomplishing tasks with the available resources while maintaining the integrity of the institution, as emphasized by Admiral William H. McRaven. This aligns with ensuring the growth and needs of team members are prioritized, creating an empowering environment where professionals feel valued and supported. Servant leadership is characterized by a focus on serving others, where a leader's primary role is to support and elevate their team members. This

DOI: 10.1201/9781003462064-6

approach is especially relevant in the high-pressure environment of cybersecurity, where the well-being and development of each team member are essential for the team's overall success. At the core of servant leadership is the idea of being there for your team members, not just as a supervisor, manager, or leader but as a coach, mentor and supporter. This involves a commitment to helping them achieve their career goals and personal aspirations. *When leaders invest time and resources in their team's growth, it not only enhances individual capabilities but also strengthens the team*. This approach fosters a community of learning and mutual support, which is vital in the constantly evolving field of cybersecurity. Stewardship is another key aspect of servant leadership. Stewardship refers to the responsibility of caring for and improving the team and its resources. In cybersecurity, stewardship means ensuring that the team has the necessary tools, training, and support to excel in their roles. This commitment to the team's well-being is crucial for retaining top talent in a field where skilled professionals are in high demand.

Engaging and developing others is at the heart of servant leadership. It's about working together to understand and shape the future of the cybersecurity landscape. By encouraging collaboration and idea-sharing, a servant leader fosters an environment where every team member feels valued and empowered to contribute. This collaborative approach is essential for staying ahead of emerging cybersecurity threats and trends. Continuous reinvestment in the team and valuing both relationships and results are fundamental to servant leadership. This means consistently looking for opportunities to enhance team capabilities and strengthen bonds among team members. In cybersecurity, where the challenges are complex and ever-changing, the strength of the team's relationships is as important as their technical skills. For a leader to effectively embody the culture and values they want to see in their team, they must first embrace these qualities themselves. This authenticity in leadership is critical for building trust and respect within the team. When team members see their leader genuinely committed to the values and culture of the organization, they are more likely to mirror these behaviors. Forming leadership teams within the cybersecurity group is also important. These teams can help disseminate the servant leadership approach throughout the organization, ensuring that the philosophy is not just top-down but is embraced at all levels. A critical aspect of servant leadership is the rejection of the blame game. In cybersecurity, where the risk of mistakes can be high, it's important to foster a culture where errors are treated as learning opportunities rather than occasions for punishment. A culture of covering up mistakes or shifting blame is destructive and undermines trust and collaboration, which are essential for having an effective cybersecurity program. Emotional intelligence, acceptance, and empathy are vital components of servant leadership. These qualities enable leaders to understand and respond to the needs and emotions of their team members, creating a supportive and understanding work environment. In cybersecurity, where stress and pressure can be high, these emotional skills are particularly valuable. Finally, the concept of Earth, Wind, Fire, and Water, as described in "Servant Leadership in Action" by Ken Blanchard, offers a framework for applying servant leadership principles. These elements represent different aspects of leadership - stability, inspiration, passion, and adaptability, respectively. In the context of cybersecurity, this means providing a stable and secure environment (Earth), inspiring the team with a clear vision (Wind), fueling their passion for the work (Fire), and being adaptable to the ever-changing cybersecurity landscape (Water). Servant leadership in cybersecurity is about putting the team first, fostering a culture of learning and support, and being committed to the growth and well-being of each team member. It's about leading by example, promoting collaboration, and building a team that is resilient, adaptable, and deeply committed to the mission. By embracing these principles, leaders can create an environment where their team not only succeeds in the present but is also prepared for the challenges of the future.

The leadership style you blend and adopt plays a crucial role in shaping the team's effectiveness and morale. Positive energy leadership, a concept well-articulated in various leadership books, is particularly relevant in the high-stress cybersecurity field. The essence of positive energy leadership is about fostering a work environment where enthusiasm, motivation, and positivity are not just encouraged, but actively practiced. This approach has a significant positive impact team morale and motivation. In cybersecurity, where the stakes are high and the pressure is constant, leading with positive energy can create a more collaborative and supportive atmosphere. It fosters a culture of growth, learning, and innovation, which are essential for staying ahead in a rapidly evolving field. Jon Gordon's work, particularly in "Stick Together" and "The Energy Bus," provides valuable insights into the power of positivity. Gordon emphasizes the importance of sticking together as a team, suggesting that a united team is a stronger team. This unity is often fostered through positive leadership. In "The Energy Bus," Gordon talks about the infectious nature of positive energy, highlighting how it can transform an organization's culture and drive. In cybersecurity, this translates into a team that is more resilient, adaptable, and committed to overcoming challenges together. Adrian Gostick's "The 24-Carrot Manager" also sheds light on the importance of recognition and appreciation in leadership. Gostick argues that recognizing and rewarding employees' efforts leads to higher engagement and productivity. In the context of cybersecurity, where the work can often be behind the scenes and thankless, acknowledging team members' contributions becomes even more critical. It's essential to regularly express gratitude, especially when someone goes above and beyond. This recognition should be sincere, as insincere praise can erode trust and undermine the team's integrity. An essential aspect of positive energy leadership is the physical presence and interaction with team members. It's crucial for leaders in cybersecurity to get out of their offices and engage with their teams personally. These interactions are opportunities to show genuine appreciation for the hard work and dedication of the team. They are also moments to reinforce the mission and the vital role each team member plays in achieving it. Drawing from Eric Harvey's "The Leadership Secrets of Santa Claus," we see the importance of loving the job and the mission. In cybersecurity, this translates to a leader who is passionate about protecting data and assets, a passion that becomes contagious among team members. In todays work landscape, getting up and out of your office can be metaphorical for those of you with global, virtual teams that are mostly remote. However, it is a leadership failure to allow that type of environment to stop you from having a presence with your team members. Harvey points out that Santa's number-one priority is his mission, and he effectively rallies his team around this mission. Similarly, a cybersecurity leader should inspire their team by demonstrating a deep commitment to the mission of safeguarding information and assets. Positive energy leadership is not just about being upbeat; it's about creating an environment where team members feel valued, appreciated, and part of something significant. It's about demonstrating genuine appreciation, recognizing efforts, and fostering a supportive and collaborative culture. This approach does not open the door to being taken advantage of; rather, it builds a strong, united team capable of facing the complex challenges inherent in cybersecurity. In a field where threats are ever-evolving and the pressure is relentless, a positive, appreciative, and mission-focused leadership style is not just beneficial but essential.

Assuming positive intent is a vital strategy in cultivating trust among team members, especially in the intricate field of cybersecurity. This approach involves giving team members the benefit of the doubt and interpreting their actions and words in positive light. When leaders and team members adopt this mindset, it creates an atmosphere of mutual respect and understanding. This perspective encourages open communication and reduces the likelihood of misunderstandings or misinterpretations that can lead to mistrust. By believing that each team member is acting with the best intentions, even when mistakes occur or when viewpoints differ, a foundation of trust is built. This trust is crucial in cybersecurity, where collaboration, rapid response to threats, and effective teamwork are essential for success. Assuming positive intent not only strengthens team cohesion but also fosters a more supportive and psychologically safe environment, where individuals feel valued and are more likely to contribute their best efforts. The concepts from "Gung Ho" by Ken Blanchard, one of the leadership books that truly laid the foundation for my style of leadership, provides valuable insights into how this might be achieved. Blanchard emphasizes the importance of making work meaningful for employees. He introduces the concept of the **'Spirit of the Squirrel,'** which is all about understanding and valuing the work's purpose. In cybersecurity, this translates to ensuring that each team member comprehends the significant impact of their role. They are not just monitoring systems or implementing protocols; they are guardians of digital safety, protecting sensitive information and assets from malicious threats. When team members grasp the broader impact of their work, their tasks become more than just a list of responsibilities; they become a mission they are passionate about. Another concept from the book is the **'Way of the Beaver,'** which is about empowering employees to take control of their work. In the context of cybersecurity, this means giving team members autonomy and the ability to make decisions within their areas of expertise. When individuals feel they have a say in how things are done and that their expertise is valued and trusted, their engagement and loyalty to the team and the mission increase significantly. The third concept, the **'Gift of the Goose,'** is about cheering each other on. In a high-pressure field like cybersecurity, *acknowledging and celebrating small victories and team efforts is essential.* It fosters a positive work environment where team members feel encouraged and supported. This encouragement is crucial for maintaining morale, especially when facing challenging situations. Applying these principles from "Gung Ho" to cybersecurity leadership can profoundly impact team dynamics. It transforms routine tasks into meaningful components of a larger mission, empowers team members to take ownership of their roles, and creates an environment of support and encouragement. When work is perceived as meaningful and fulfilling, it naturally sustains interest, ignites passion, and strengthens loyalty. This approach is particularly effective in cybersecurity, where the nature of the work can be intense and demanding. By adopting these principles, leaders can ensure that their teams not only remain engaged and committed but also find satisfaction and purpose in their work.

Trust-based leadership fosters a stronger, more loyal team, as professionals feel confident, they can rely on their leaders for support and guidance. This kind of leadership promotes transparency and open communication, leading to better collaboration and a more productive work environment. The principles drawn from Ken Blanchard's "Trust Works," Stephen M.R. Covey's "The Speed of Trust," Admiral William H. McRaven's "The Wisdom of Bullfrog Leadership," and Eric Harvey's "The Leadership Secrets of Santa Claus" provide a comprehensive framework for building this trust. Being present and listening to team members is a cornerstone of trust-based leadership, as highlighted in Harvey's work. It's about understanding their perspectives, challenges, and ideas in cybersecurity, where each detail can have significant implications. When team members feel genuinely heard, they're more engaged and invested in their work. Walking the talk, as Covey and Blanchard suggest, is another key aspect. Cybersecurity leaders must embody the principles of integrity and security they advocate. Keep in mind that for many team members your actions will speak louder to them then your words do. Consistently demonstrating these values builds credibility and trust within the team. McRaven's concept of daring leadership, involving bold action and preparedness, is also crucial for building trust. In cybersecurity, this means being ready to tackle challenges head-on, while also empowering the team to take calculated risks. Accountability is a cornerstone of any high-functioning cybersecurity team, but it must be framed as an opportunity for growth rather than a vehicle for blame. Mistakes should be seen as steppingstones for learning and improvement, fostering a culture of continuous innovation. In cybersecurity, where challenges are complex and evolving, this mindset encourages resilience and adaptability. Recognizing when projects are "Red", struggling or at risk, is not a sign of failure but an opportunity for intervention. When leaders step in to provide support, collaborate, and find solutions, they not only resolve the immediate issue but also strengthen the team's problem-solving abilities and confidence. These moments build the foundation for a culture of transparency and mutual trust. Escalating issues for help should never be seen as a negative act, provided the intention is to seek guidance, not to pass off responsibilities. Escalations are often a vital component of teamwork, reflecting a collaborative effort to overcome challenges and achieve shared goals. They demonstrate that the individual values the success of the team and the organization over personal pride. Leaders must also lead by example in accountability. Owning up to their mistakes, especially in cases of leadership missteps, sets a powerful precedent for the team. This kind of self-accountability reinforces trust, models integrity, and underscores the importance of holding oneself to the same standards expected of others. Finally, building trust and a culture of accountability begins with ensuring the right team members are in place, individuals who are both skilled and aligned with the organization's mission. These elements, working together, create an environment where accountability drives growth, trust, and collective success. It's about ensuring the team comprises individuals who are skilled, committed, and aligned with the organization's values and mission. This alignment is essential for a cohesive and effective team.

Maintaining a professional, respectful work environment is non-negotiable in any high-performing cybersecurity team. Unprofessional behavior, such as gossiping, bad-mouthing colleagues, or undermining other leaders or teams, must be addressed swiftly and decisively. A culture of respect and integrity requires zero tolerance for such conduct, as it erodes trust, collaboration, and the very foundation of team culture. Healthy teams thrive on dissenting opinions and open discussions, where ideas are debated openly, and differences of opinion are welcomed as opportunities for growth and innovation. However, when conversations become muted, secretive, or occur in hushed tones because individuals feel guilty or unsure about the negativity of their remarks, the situation has already veered into unhealthy territory. Such behavior poisons the team culture and creates an undercurrent of mistrust and divisiveness. Addressing this requires courage and maturity from all team members. As discussed in *Difficult Conversations* by Douglas Stone, Bruce Patton, and Sheila Heen, challenging topics should be approached through adult, constructive dialogue. Individuals must be encouraged to voice their concerns openly and respectfully, focusing on solutions rather than perpetuating negativity. Leaders, in turn, must foster an environment where such conversations can occur safely and productively. For those unwilling to address their concerns constructively or who persist in covert negativity, it may be time for a candid conversation about their fit within the team. *Negative attitudes that linger and spread unaddressed can sabotage the morale and effectiveness of the entire group. Sometimes, the best course of action is to ask these individuals to find a "different bus to ride," ensuring their behavior does not derail the broader team's success.* Creating and sustaining a positive focus on strategy and mission is central to a trust-centered culture. This involves avoiding workplace politics and shifting the team's energy toward achieving shared goals. Trust-centered leadership, as emphasized by Blanchard, Covey, McRaven, and Harvey, incorporates active listening, leading by example, handling mistakes constructively, supporting team members during challenges, maintaining accountability, and always ensuring professionalism. When issues impacting team culture are identified, they must be prioritized and resolved immediately. Team dynamics are the lifeblood of a cybersecurity organization and neglecting them can have far-reaching, negative consequences. By addressing negativity openly, modeling constructive behavior, and maintaining a steadfast focus on collaboration and respect, leaders can create a resilient, unified, and high-performing team capable of navigating the ever-changing complexities of cybersecurity.

Exceptional leadership in cybersecurity extends beyond the technical aspects of managing threats and risks. It is deeply rooted in principles that inspire, motivate, and support team members in their professional journeys. Effective leaders prioritize servant leadership, cultivate positive energy, and foster a culture of trust that serves as the foundation for a resilient and high-performing team. Servant leadership stands out as a transformative philosophy, emphasizing the importance of placing the growth and well-being of the team above personal ambition. Leaders who adopt this approach act as mentors and stewards, ensuring that team members have the tools, training, and support they need to succeed. This focus on stewardship, caring for the team and its resources, fosters an environment where professionals feel valued and empowered to excel. In a field as dynamic and demanding as cybersecurity, where challenges are both complex and evolving, this investment in people strengthens not only individual capabilities but also the collective resilience of the team. Trust emerges as another cornerstone of effective leadership. Building trust requires consistent actions, transparency, and a willingness to lead by example. Leaders earn trust by demonstrating emotional intelligence, maintaining authenticity, and providing constructive feedback. When mistakes occur, treating them as learning opportunities rather than failures encourages innovation and continuous improvement. A culture of openness, where team members feel safe to voice concerns and share ideas, creates a collaborative environment essential for addressing cybersecurity's unpredictable challenges. Positive energy leadership complements these efforts by fostering an atmosphere of optimism, enthusiasm, and motivation. In high-pressure environments, maintaining positivity helps alleviate stress and encourages creative problem-solving. Recognizing and celebrating achievements, whether individual or team-based, reinforces a sense of purpose and builds morale. Leaders who engage authentically with their teams by listening to concerns, showing appreciation, and reinforcing the mission create an environment where people feel inspired to give their best.

Professionalism and respect are non-negotiable elements of a healthy team culture. Negative behaviors, such as gossip, hidden conversations, or undermining colleagues, erode trust and harm team dynamics. Constructive and open dialogue is critical for resolving issues and fostering mutual respect. When individuals persist in fostering negativity without addressing concerns through direct, adult conversations, their impact must be addressed swiftly to protect the integrity of the team. Ensuring that dissenting opinions are expressed constructively promotes a culture of accountability and continuous improvement, while harmful negativity should lead to reassessment of team roles. A shared mission and clear objectives provide a unifying vision, ensuring that all efforts align with the broader goals of the organization. A simple, memorable mission statement reinforces purpose and direction, while actionable team principles keep the focus on what truly matters. These principles should enhance the organization's overarching mission, never detract from it, creating alignment between daily efforts and strategic objectives Leaders must also embrace accountability as a critical component of a thriving team culture. Addressing mistakes constructively, stepping in to support struggling projects, and modeling self-accountability set the tone for a transparent and trustworthy environment. Escalating issues when necessary is not a failure but a function of teamwork, seeking help to overcome challenges collaboratively strengthens the team's capacity to achieve mutual success. Ultimately, the most effective leaders recognize that cybersecurity is as much about people as it is about technology. Empowering individuals, fostering trust, and creating a positive, professional environment ensures that teams are equipped not only to meet current challenges but also to adapt and thrive in the face of future uncertainties. Leadership rooted in these principles builds teams that are resilient, innovative, and deeply committed to the shared mission of safeguarding the organization.

Chapter 6 Notable passages and key points

- *"Servant leadership in cybersecurity is about putting the team first, fostering a culture of learning and support, and being committed to the growth and well-being of each team member. By being there for team members as mentors and supporters, leaders create an environment where every individual feels valued, empowered to contribute, and aligned with the mission. This approach not only enhances individual capabilities but strengthens the team as a whole, making it essential in the constantly evolving field of cybersecurity."*
- *"A critical aspect of servant leadership is the rejection of the blame game, especially important in cybersecurity where the risk of mistakes can be high. By treating errors as learning opportunities*

rather than occasions for punishment, leaders foster a culture of continuous improvement and collaboration. This mindset, coupled with emotional intelligence, acceptance, and empathy, creates a supportive work environment. These qualities enable leaders to effectively respond to the needs and emotions of their team members, which is invaluable in managing the stress and pressure inherent in cybersecurity."

- **Servant Leadership**: Prioritizing team growth and support builds trust and fosters resilience to meet cybersecurity challenges.
- **Positive Energy**: Inspiring collaboration and morale through optimism and recognition enhances team effectiveness.
- **Building Trust**: Authenticity and empathy strengthen communication and alignment in tackling cybersecurity threats.

7

Bonus Thoughts

Advanced Leadership Tools and Concepts

- **Psychological Safety in Team Communications**: If team members frequently CC you and others on most emails, it's a red flag for a psychological safety issue. This behavior often stems from a need to "cover their backs," indicating a lack of trust or fear of repercussions. As a leader, it's crucial to address this immediately. Investigate the root causes and work to create an environment where team members feel secure and trusted without the need for constant oversight.
- **Effective Email Communication (BLUF Principle)**: Emphasize the importance of the 'Bottom Line Up Front' (BLUF) in emails. In a world flooded with electronic communication, it's essential to be concise and clear. Start emails with the main point or request, followed by necessary details. This approach respects everyone's time and ensures that key messages are not lost in unnecessary verbosity.
- **Handling Defensive Situations**: Composing a lengthy, defensive email may feel satisfying in the moment, but it rarely leads to positive outcomes. If you catch yourself drafting a multi-page response to defend your position, pause, reflect, and consider setting it aside. Taking a defensive tone often escalates tensions and detracts from resolving the issue at hand. Early in my career, I struggled with this, driven by a desire to showcase my value to my leaders and wanted to make sure they knew the mistake was not mine. However, I eventually learned that the most effective approach is not to dwell on justifying past actions but to focus on constructive, collaborative, and forward-thinking solutions. Shifting the conversation toward what can be achieved, rather than what went wrong, fosters better understanding, builds trust, and

DOI: 10.1201/9781003462064-7

moves the team toward resolution. I recently received a very long and technically detailed email explaining why someone was right and I was wrong. It was so long I couldn't make it through the entire email. My response back was simply, "Well thought out and well said." That spurred the person to give me a phone call to see if I actually agreed with them. The phone call lead to a very good conversation and resulted in a win-win solution.

Tips and Hints for Building Team Unity and Recognition in Cybersecurity

- **Team Challenge Coins**: Consider issuing challenge coins to your team members. They serve as a symbol of unity and can be shared with supporters of your cybersecurity efforts. Hosting an annual design competition for these coins can also enhance engagement and creativity.
- **Team Mascot Patch**: Adopt a team mascot and create a patch that all members can wear or put on their backpacks. For external collaborators, consider designing a different colored patch to recognize their contributions.
- **Unit Patches**: If your organization has various teams, like threat hunters or operations, encourage them to design their own patches. This can foster a sense of identity and creativity within each unit.
- **Custom Patches for CIRT Members**: Create custom patches for each major event for your Cybersecurity Incident Response Team members that worked the CIRT. These can be symbols of achievement and pride.
- **Military Style Backpacks**: As a recognition tool, provide military-style backpacks to your team members. They can use these to display their team and unit patches, enhancing a sense of belonging.
- **Annual Wargames and Virtual Learning Escape Rooms**: Regularly conduct wargames and virtual learning escape rooms to build skills and strengthen team bonds.
- **New Hire Welcome Box**: Give new hires a welcome box with items that reflect your team's culture, such as a challenge coin,

team mascot patch, and a welcome letter. Include materials like the book "How Full Is Your Bucket" to introduce them to the team's values and history.

Creating a clear, memorable mission statement for your cybersecurity team is a powerful tool for unifying efforts and aligning everyone's focus on shared goals. While this team-centric mission should provide clarity and direction for daily activities, it must in no way detract from or conflict with the broader organizational mission statement. Instead, it should serve as a supportive, reinforcing element that helps team members connect their work to the overarching goals of the organization. For example, a succinct team mission statement might be: *"We protect the organization's data and assets."* This simple declaration captures the essence of the team's role and ensures that every member remains grounded in their primary purpose. In addition to the mission statement, selecting a few core principles for team members to internalize can further enhance focus and accountability. These principles should be easy to remember and actionable, guiding behavior and decision-making in a practical way. Examples include:

- *"What have you improved today to protect the organization's data and assets?"* This encourages a proactive mindset and a commitment to continuous improvement.
- *"Stay productive, not busy."* A reminder to prioritize meaningful work that directly contributes to the team's mission.
- *"Are you doing the little things right?"* Reinforcing the importance of attention to detail, which is critical in maintaining strong cybersecurity practices.

These guiding statements help instill a sense of purpose and accountability in every team member. By anchoring individual contributions to both the team's mission and the organization's broader objectives, leaders foster alignment, engagement, and a shared commitment to success.

Bibliography

Blanchard, K., & Hodges, P. (2003). *Servant leadership in action: How you can achieve great relationships and results*. HarperCollins.

Blanchard, K., & Johnson, S. (2015). *The new one-minute manager*. William Morrow.

Blanchard, K., Carlos, J., & Randolph, A. (2001). *Empowerment takes more than a minute*. Berrett-Koehler Publishers.

Blanchard, K., Lacinak, T., Tompkins, C., & Ballard, K. (2003). *Whale done! The power of positive relationships*. Free Press.

Blanchard, K., Miller, M., & Oncken, W. (2000). *The one-minute manager meets the monkey*. William Morrow.

Blanchard, K., & Stoner, J. (2003). *Gung Ho! Turn on the people in any organization*. HarperBusiness.

Blanchard, K., Ridge, R., & Highsmith, M. (2016). *The servant leadership handbook: Achieving great relationships and results*. HarperCollins.

Covey, S. R. (1989). *The 7 habits of highly effective people: Powerful lessons in personal change*. Free Press.

Covey, S. M. R., & Merrill, R. R. (2006). *The speed of trust: The one thing that changes everything*. Free Press.

Covey, S. R., McChesney, C., & Huling, S. (2012). *The four disciplines of execution: Achieving your wildly important goals*. Free Press.

Covey, S. M. R. (2013). *Trust works: Four keys to building lasting relationships*. Free Press.

Dweck, C. (2006). *Mindset: The new psychology of success*. Random House.

Farber, S. (2004). *Radical leap: A personal lesson in extreme leadership*. Kaplan Business.

Farber, S. (2009). *Greater than yourself: The ultimate lesson of true leadership*. Doubleday.

Farber, S. (2017). *Love is just damn good business: Do what you love in the service of people who love what you do*. Wiley.

Gordon, J. (2007). *The energy bus: 10 rules to fuel your life, work, and team with positive energy*. Wiley.

Gordon, J., & Smith, D. (2021). *Stick together: A simple lesson to build a stronger team*. Wiley.

Gostick, A., & Elton, C. (2002). *The 24-carrot manager: A remarkable story of how a leader can unleash human potential*. Wiley.

Harvey, E. (2003). *The leadership secrets of Santa Claus: How to get big things done in YOUR "workshop"... all year long*. Simple Truths.

Katzenbach, J. R., & Smith, D. K. (1993a). *The discipline of teams: A mind to lead*. Harvard Business Review Press.

Katzenbach, J. R., & Smith, D. K. (1993b). *The wisdom of teams: Creating the high-performance organization*. Harvard Business Review Press.

Liker, J. K., & Meier, D. (2007). *Toyota talent: Developing your people the Toyota way*. McGraw-Hill.

Liker, J. K., & Ogden, T. N. (2011). *The Toyota way to continuous improvement: Linking strategy and operational excellence to achieve superior performance*. McGraw-Hill.

McLaughlin, K. L. (n.d.). *Cybersecurity talent retention strategies: Building winning teams*. [Unpublished manuscript].

McRaven, W. H. (2022). *The wisdom of bullfrog leadership: Lessons in life and leadership*. Grand Central Publishing.

Patterson, K., Grenny, J., McMillan, R., & Switzler, A. (2011). *Crucial conversations: Tools for talking when stakes are high*. McGraw-Hill Education.

Senn, L., & Hart, J. (2013). *Winning teams, winning cultures*. Wiley.

Senn, L. (2006). *The mood elevator: Take charge of your feelings, become a better you*. McGraw-Hill.

Smith, D. (2013a). *The monk and the Ferrari: The art of living with balance, purpose, and joy*. Harmony.

Smith, J. (2013b). *The sale: A journey of leadership and purpose*. Harmony.

Strelecky, J. (2007). *The why café*. Da Capo Lifelong Books.

Strelecky, J. (2010). *Return to the why café*. Da Capo Lifelong Books.

Waldrop, T. (2019). *Cybersecurity metrics: A practical framework for measuring security & protecting data*. Wiley.

$(ISC)^2$. (2022). *Cybersecurity workforce study*. $(ISC)^2$.

For Product Safety Concerns and Information please contact our EU
representative GPSR@taylorandfrancis.com
Taylor & Francis Verlag GmbH, Kaufingerstraße 24, 80331 München, Germany

www.ingramcontent.com/pod-product-compliance
Ingram Content Group UK Ltd.
Pitfield, Milton Keynes, MK11 3LW, UK
UKHW020157260926
475702UK00047B/672
* 9 7 8 1 0 3 2 6 1 1 0 9 9 *